King Arthur

A Pantomime Adventure in Camelot

Paul Reakes

Samuel French — London
New York - Toronto - Hollywood

CHARACTERS

King Arthur of Camelot
Queen Guinevere, his wife
Merlin, the court wizard
Sir Lancelot
Squirt, his squire
Olivia, a lady-in-waiting
Morgana, an evil sorceress
Mordred, her son
Sally Simple, a kitchen maid
Smoulder, a small dragon
A Large Dragon
A Page

Chorus of: **Knights**, **Ladies of the Court**, **Servants**, **Demons**, **Zombies** and **Ghouls**

SYNOPSIS OF SCENES

PROLOGUE

ACT I

SCENE I   The Courtyard of Camelot
SCENE 2   Outside the Castle Walls
SCENE 3   The Jousting Tournament
SCENE 4   Outside the Castle Walls
SCENE 5   The Enchanted Forest

ACT II

SCENE 1   The Banqueting Hall of Camelot
SCENE 2   Outside the Castle Walls
SCENE 3   The Royal Bedchamber
SCENE 4   On the Edge of the Enchanted Forest
SCENE 5   The Gateway to Morgana's Castle
SCENE 6   A Little Knight Music
SCENE 7   The Grand Finale

MUSICAL PLOT

ACT I

1	**Song and Dance**	Sally, Chorus and Dancers
2	**Comedy Song**	Guinevere
3	**Song and Dance**	Guinevere, Arthur, Squirt, Smoulder and Chorus
4	**Duet**	Lancelot and Olivia
5	**Comedy Song and Dance**	Squirt, Sally and Smoulder
6	**Song and Dance**	Chorus and Dancers
7	**Song and Dance**	Principals, Chorus and Dancers
8	**Song and Dance**	Chorus and Dancers
9	**Duet and Dance**	Morgana, Mordred, Chorus and Dancers

ACT II

10	**Song and Dance**	Principals, Chorus and Dancers
11	**Duet**	Lancelot and Olivia
12	**Comedy Duet**	Squirt and Sally
13	**Comic Striptease**	Guinevere
14	**Ghouls Dance**	Dancers and Chorus
15	**Song and Dance**	Principals, Chorus and Dancers
16	**House Song**	Guinevere, Squirt, Sally, Smoulder and Audience
17	**Finale Song**	All

CHARACTERS AND COSTUMES

King Arthur, in this tale, is not the popular conception of the great hero of myth and legend. He is a cheerful chump in the old fashioned "Silly Ass" mode. Imagine P. G. Wodehouse's Bertie Wooster as King of the Britons and you'll get the idea. He is very affable and regards everyone, including the audience, as his "Jolly Old Chums". He is involved in plenty of audience participation and provides much of the comedy. His regal costumes should be a comical mixture of 1920s and Arthurian. No whiskers, please! Facial hair would not be in keeping with his type of character. A monocle, however, would certainly be! Finale Costume.

Queen Guinevere (Dame) is also the complete opposite to the accepted idea of Camelot's beautiful and gracious monarch. With a huge stretch of the imagination you might think that she was once a beauty — but! She enjoys being royal, tries to be ultra posh, but is really as common as muck! With all her faults she is still a loveable old girl. She is on friendly and confidential terms with the audience, especially the females. Her make-up, hair and regal costumes are always outrageous and funny. Special Finale Costume.

Merlin is the Court Wizard, General Factotum and long suffering advisor to King Arthur. He is a wise old bird, still spry and always speaks in rhyme. Although completely loyal and devoted to the 'Royals', he is constantly irritated by their inept behaviour and makes no pretence of his feelings, particularly to the audience. He has long white hair, and a white beard that nearly touches the ground. He wears the pointed wizard's hat and flowing gown decorated with magical symbols. He is never without his magic wand, which takes the form of a tall, curiously twisted, staff.

Sir Lancelot (Principal Boy) is everything you would expect a gallant Knight of the Round Table to be. He is young, handsome, charming and chivalrous. Not only is he a wonderful warrior, he can sing and dance brilliantly as well! All his costumes are magnificent, and show off his figure and shapely legs to perfection. Finale Costume.

Squirt is Lancelot's Squire. Not over burdened with brains, he is an extremely likeable young buffoon who instantly makes friends with the audience, especially the youngsters. He is always at the mercy of his love-sick girlfriend Sally, but is not adverse to making fun of her. He is involved in plenty of audience participation and comic capers. Singing and dancing ability an advantage. Comical costumes with ill-fitting tights, etc. and a very short night-shirt in Act II. Finale Costume.

Olivia (Principal Girl) is the beautiful young lady-in-waiting to Queen Guinevere. She is charm itself, and is never soppy or simpering. It goes without saying that Lancelot falls in love with her the moment they meet, and who could blame him? Singing and dancing ability is needed. All of her costumes are exquisite. Finale Costume.

Morgana is the Evil Sorceress to end all evil sorceresses! She is an out-and-out nasty who uses all her diabolical powers to overthrow Arthur and become ruler of Britain. She never misses an opportunity of goading the audience into a frenzy of boos and hisses. She only shows a lighter side when dealing with her son, Mordred. But even that is short-lived! Magnificently evil black costumes, with bizarre make-up and head dress.

Mordred is Morgana's son. Although menacing and evil in appearance, he is really a weak, cowardly "Mummy's Boy". He enjoys sneering at the others and goading the audience, but only when Mummy is there to protect him. Evil black costume with cloak.

Sally is the buxom kitchen maid and girlfriend of Squirt. She is madly in love with him, obsessed with marriage and anything but gentle in her show of affections. She is involved in the audience participation and comic capers. A comedienne's part with singing and dancing ability an advantage. Comical kitchen costumes with cap and apron, etc. and a ludicrous pink pyjama suit in Act II. Finale Costume.

Smoulder (female or child's part) is a baby dragon. She is very cute and soon becomes a favourite with the audience, especially the youngsters. For a dragon she is no mean dancer, and enjoys giving Squirt and Sally the run around. Her appearance may be a departure from the usual pantomime "animals", but the ingenuity of costume designers is incredible! Perhaps a little fancy ruff for the Finale.

A Large Dragon that turns out to be Smoulder's mother! She is huge, fearsome and capable of breathing fire (fortunately off stage!) She must not be played as a Chinese Dragon. This is a one person species and played in the manner of a Tyrannosaurus Rex. Persuade the tallest person you can find to undertake the role. With an extended neck and headpiece, the Dragon should then tower over everyone else. Again your costume designer will work wonders! It is advisable to have this costume well in use before the actual performance. Perhaps a little flowered hat for the Finale.

The Page (child's part) is totally "laid back", has no respect for anyone, and suffers from a permanent loud sniff! Page costume, wig, tights, etc.

The Chorus, Dancers and Children appear as Knights, Court Ladies, their children, Heralds, Servants, Vendors, Tumblers, Demons and Ghouls. All participate in the action and musical numbers.

PRODUCTION NOTES

Staging

The pantomime offers opportunities for elaborate staging, but can be produced quite simply if facilities and funds are limited. There are five full sets: The Courtyard of Camelot (this can be used for the Finale), the Jousting Tournament, The Enchanted Forest, The Banqueting Hall of Camelot and The Gateway to Morgana's Castle. There is one half set: The Royal Bedchamber. These scenes are interlinked with tabs or frontcloth scenes.

Excalibur

It goes without saying that this must be a very impressive looking sword. Handsomely wrought and bejewelled, it stands taller than the Page who carries it. It should be made from a light material, remembering that a child has to hold it upright for quite long periods. Arthur must give the impression that it weighs a ton.

The Joust

The red and black armour. This should not present a problem to your ingenious costume designer! It can be as elaborate as you can make it, resembling either plate armour or chain mail. The latter will probably be easier to reproduce. The helmets should have large plumes.

The horses. These are 'worn' by the actors playing Lancelot And Mordred, who use their own legs to simulate the 'horse's' movements. They should be constructed on light frames with only tails and armoured heads showing. The rest of the 'horse', and the actor's lower half, is concealed by a long decorative 'skirt'. False legs can be made to hang on either side of the 'horse'. It is advisable to have the 'horses' well in use before the actual performance.

The lances. Obviously these should be made in accordance with the stage space available.

PROLOGUE

After the Overture, there is a flash, a puff of smoke and Merlin appears in front of the main curtain, DR. *He stands in a spotlight and "magical" music plays softly under his following speech*

Coughing and spluttering, he waves the smoke away, peers out at the audience and greets them

Merlin　　　　Warm welcome and greetings to one and all.
　　　　　　　Be you long in the tooth or just learnt to crawl!
　　　　　　　This hat and this wand my business proclaim,
　　　　　　　I am a wizard and Merlin is my name.
　　　　　　　Long years ago when my beard was half grown,
　　　　　　　There stood on a hill a great slab of stone.
　　　　　　　Fixed in that rock was the sword Excalibur,
　　　　　　　A wondrous blade of magical calibre!
　　　　　　　"Whoever can pull the sword from the stone,
　　　　　　　He will be king and shall sit on the throne!"
　　　　　　　Many men tried, they came by the hoard,
　　　　　　　But none could remove that magical sword!
　　　　　　　Then up stepped a boy, no more than a sprout,
　　　　　　　And without hesitation he pulled the sword out!
　　　　　　　That's how young Arthur became the true king,
　　　　　　　And soon all Britain his praises would sing!
　　　　　　　He built a fine castle that shone in the sun
　　　　　　　(It's open to the public from ten until one!)
　　　　　　　He gathered around him an army of knights,
　　　　　　　Who rescued fair damsels and looked good in tights!
　　　　　　　All of these knights were brave, pure and true,
　　　　　　　(But there was the odd dirty knight between me and you!)
　　　　　　　For these gallant fellows he built a round table,
　　　　　　　And at it they'd sit drinking Carling Black Label!
　　　　　　　When Arthur asked Guinevere to be his queen
　　　　　　　She was the loveliest girl he ever had seen.
　　　　　　　But if only he had seen her mother before,
　　　　　　　He'd have known what the future had in store!
　　　　　　　Enough of this preamble and on with the plot!
　　　　　　　Prepare to enter King Arthur's Court—at stately *Camelot*!

Grandly, he waves his wand at the main curtain

    There is a flash, a puff of smoke and Merlin disappears, DR

A fanfare is played, and the CURTAIN *rises on* ——

ACT I

SCENE 1

The Courtyard of Camelot

Sky blue cyclorama. A raised walk across the back with battlements and steps down. At the sides are castle walls with small turrets down R and L

The Chorus and Dancers as Knights, Court Ladies, Servants, etc. are discovered. Sally Simple can be with them or can enter after the number. They all go straight into a colourful and lively opening song and dance

Song 1

After the song, Sally rushes forward or runs on, excitedly

Sally (*to the others*) Is it true? *Is it true?* Oh, *please* tell me it's true!
Knight Be calm, Sally. Is *what* true?
Sally Is Sir Lancelot returnin' from 'is quest today?
Lady I've not heard that, but I sincerely hope so.
2nd Lady Indeed. His handsome face and charming manner has been sorely missed here in Camelot.
All Women (*sighing*) Oh! Dear Sir Lancelot!
Sally Oh, it ain't Lancelot I'm dyin' to see! It's 'is Squirt!
All His *what*?
Sally 'Is Squirt! 'Is squire — Squirt!
All Oh, Squirt, the squire!
Sally Yes! 'E promised we'd get engaged as soon as 'e got back from the quest! (*All soppy*) 'E's going' to ask for my 'and!
Knight And nothing else?

He and the others roar with laughter

Sally (*getting in a huff*) Well? Is 'e comin' back today or ain't 'e?
Knight We know not, girl. (*He looks off R*) Ah! Here comes Merlin. Ask him. He's bound to know.

Merlin enters from R

Sally rushes straight to him and starts pulling at his gown

Sally Is it true? Oh, *please, please* tell me it's true!
Merlin   Desist at once from pulling at my clothes!
                           If you don't, who knows what you might expose!
Sally (*letting go of him*) Is Sir Lancelot comin' back today? Please tell me!
  Is 'e?
Merlin   This question seems to cause you stress!
                           The answer is quite simply — Yes!
Sally (*over the moon*) Hurray!

In her joy she kisses Merlin

He reacts, and the others roar with laughter

Merlin   Away with you girl! Get back to your baking!
                           An important announcement I should be making!
Sally (*skipping with joy and weaving in and out of the Chorus*) 'E's coming
  back today! Oo! My Squirty's coming 'ome! Oh, I'm so excited! Oo! I
  can't wait to see 'im!

She skips out L

*The others find this very amusing, until Merlin bangs his wand on the ground
and calls them to order*

Merlin   Pay heed all ye dwellers of fair Camelot!
                           This way comes the king you all love a lot.
                           His royal presence is now close at hand,
                           So show some respect, and strike up the band!

There is a fanfare

The Chorus move quickly to the sides and face US *in readiness. Merlin moves
down*

  *Nonchalantly, a small Page enters on the raised walk and comes down the
  steps. Upright before him, and with apparent ease, he carries the great
  sword Excalibur. He stands to one side of the steps and gives a loud sniff*

                           Behold Excalibur! King Arthur's sword!
                           Closely followed by your sovereign lord!

A louder fanfare

With the exception of the Page, all bow and curtsy US. *No-one appears! They raise their heads and look at each other in puzzlement*

The Page gives a loud sniff

Merlin clears his throat and repeats, louder

> Behold Excalibur! King Arthur's sword!
> *Closely followed by your sovereign lord!*

An even louder fanfare

All bow and curtsy as before. Again no-one appears! The Chorus look up and start giggling. Merlin turns away in agitation. The Page saunters down to him

Page Oy! Fungus face!

Merlin reacts

'Is nibbs said 'e might be a bit late 'cos the queen's took 'im shoppin' wiv 'er!

He gives a sniff and returns to the steps

Merlin (*to the audience*)
> Really! This is most frustrating!
> A king shouldn't keep his subjects waiting!

Arthur (*off, calling*) What ho!
Page 'Ere 'e is now.

King Arthur enters on the raised walk. He gives a cheery wave to the Chorus

Arthur What ho, my jolly old subjects! How absolutely spiffin' to see you all again, what! Haw! Haw! Haw!

He descends the steps and comes DS, *shaking hands with the Chorus on the way*

Hallo, old fruit! What ho, old bean! Hallo, old top! What ho, old thing! Hallo, old...

He has reached the stone-faced Merlin and reacts

Old Merlin! And how's my favourite wizard this morning? Just come out for a... *spell*, have you? Haw! Haw! Haw! (*He catches sight of the audience*) I say! By Jove! We've got some more of those jolly old visitors in the castle! (*To Merlin*) Does one talk to them, d'you think?

Merlin nods

Jolly good! (*To the audience*) What ho! (*To Merlin*) I say, I think they've dozed off! I'll have another bash. (*To the audience, louder*) What ho!

The audience shout back

Oh, awfully good! Haw! Haw! Well, my name is Arthur and I'm the king of Camelot and what not! I'd like to welcome you all to the castle, and I hope you have a frightfully jolly time viewin' my royal seat! I'm sure I can trust you lot. Not like those beastly blighters we had from (*nearby town or village*) last week! They made off with three suits of armour, the portcullis and Guinevere's old chastity belt! Absolute rotters!

Merlin   Sire, I notice there is something amiss.
                  The queen is not here. Is there a reason for this?
Arthur Yes, there jolly well is, old fruit! I've given her the slip. She's been draggin' me around the beastly shops all mornin'! My jolly old feet and ears, to say nothin' of my wallet, need a rest!
Guinevere (*off, bellowing*) Arthur? Where are you? Arthur?
Arthur (*cringing*) Oh, crickey! There she is! Quick Merlin! Make me invisible or somethin'!

Merlin raises his wand and makes ready to cast a spell

Queen Guinevere enters on the raised walk. She is followed by Olivia, carrying a bulging shopping bag

Guinevere Ah! There you are!
Arthur (*cringing*) Oh! Dash it! Too late!

Guinevere storms down to Arthur, followed by Olivia

Guinevere (*fuming*) Where 'ave you been?
Arthur H — Hallo, Guinie! I say! You're looking lovelier by the minute, old thing.
Guinevere Stop statin' the obvious! And *don't* call me old thing! How dare you run off like that! (*To the audience*) 'Usbands! Who'd 'ave 'em! There

I was, stood standin' in (*local shop*)! I turned round to ask 'is advice, an' there 'e was — *gone*! Oh! I felt a proper twerp! All the other customers started laughin' at me! *Me*, Queen Guinevere! (*To Arthur, rounding on him*) Is that what you want? Me to be a subject of reticule, an' be made a laughin' frock! Is that what you want?

Arthur (*aside*) Can't go against nature, old dear.

Guinevere What!

Arthur Er… I said, the air is very clear here, dear.

Guinevere Blow the air! What about an explanation? Why did you run off an' leave me in that humidifyin' position?

Arthur Well, I… I…

Guinevere (*arms folded*) I'm waitin'!

Arthur (*appealing to Merlin*) I… I…

Merlin   If Your Majesty pleases, the facts I can relate.
                              His majesty was called away, on an urgent matter of state.

Guinevere (*turning away, the wind taken out of her sails*) Oh! I see.

Arthur (*aside to Merlin, shaking his hand*) Well done, old boy! I owe you one! (*To Guinevere*) There you are old thing. (*Puffing out his chest*) I was called away on an urgent statter of mate — I mean matter of state!

Guinevere Right! Now that you're 'ere, I want you to 'elp choose the welcome 'ome present for Sir Lancelot.

Arthur (*whining*) Oh, dash it all! Do I have to?

Guinevere (*bellowing at him*) Yes, you do!

Arthur (*to the audience*) Looks like I have to!

Guinevere You'll be pleased to see 'im come back won't you? I thought Lancelot was your favourite knight.

Arthur Oh no! Friday night is my favourite night! Top of the Pops! (*This can be changed to suit*) Haw! Haw! Haw!

Guinevere (*to the audience*) D'you know, if wit were dynamite 'e wouldn't 'ave enough to blow 'is crown off! (*To Arthur*) Let me show you what I've got.

Arthur (*pretending to be shocked*) Oh, I say, old thing! Not in front of all these people! I mean, what have the poor souls ever done to you?

Guinevere The *presents*, you silly… sovereign you! Lady Olivia!

Olivia (*stepping forward and curtsying*) Yes, Your Majesty.

Guinevere Show the king what you've got ——

Arthur (*ogling Olivia and nudging Merlin*) I say! This is more like it!

Guinevere (*after giving Arthur an icy glare*) — in the bag!

Olivia holds the bag open for Guinevere

Now! I bought these few things at (*local store*)! They've got a special offer on this week. Yes! They'll pay *you* to take anythin' away! And that includes (*shopkeeper or assistant*)! But I can't decide which one to give to Lancelot. (*To the audience*) I mean, what can you give to the man who has everything?

Arthur A woman who wants nothing! Ta ra!

Guinevere I'll give *you* a thick ear in a minute! First, I've got this — (*she takes a large oilcan from the bag*) he can use it if he gets took short when 'e's wearing 'is armour. Or this — (*she takes out a large pair of knitting needles and a length of thick chain*) 'e can knit 'imself a new pair of chainmail Y fronts! Or this — (*she takes out a can of spray polish*) to give 'is Lance a nice shine! It says — (*reading the can*) "If your Lance is bent askew. A squirt of this and it'll be just like new"! (*To Arthur*) I think I'll try some of that on you! Or this — (*she takes out a large tin opener*) in case the oilcan doesn't work! Well, which one shall I give to Lancelot?

Arthur (*to the audience*) They're not awfully nice presents, are they?

"No" from audience

Guinevere (*to the audience*) Oh, yes they are!

Routine with audience

(*Then to Arthur, in a huff*) Well, you think of somethin', Mr Clever Clogs! You're supposed to be the Great King Arthur! The one who pulled the sword from the stone!

Arthur I jolly well did to! By the way, where *is* my sword?

The Page moves behind Arthur and gives a loud sniff, making the king jump

(*Jumping*) Ahh! Ah! There it is! Good old Excalibur! My trusty blade!

Guinevere (*to the audience*) The last time 'e used that Barbara Cartland was in the brownies!

Arthur (*to the Page, striking a very macho pose and putting on a deep voice*) Give me Excalibur!

Page You sure? (*Sniff*)

Arthur (*as himself*) Absolutely! (*Again with the pose and voice*) Give me Excalibur!

Page Well don't blame me! (*Sniff*)

Arthur (*as himself*) Give it to me at once, and stop that frightful sniffin'! You'll make the blade go all rusty!

With a shrug, the Page hands the sword to Arthur. Immediately after he takes it, the point of the blade crashes to the ground. Comic contortions as Arthur struggles and strains to lift the sword from the ground. Merlin turns away in embarrassment, and the Chorus start to giggle

Guinevere (*to the audience*) 'E can't get it up!
Arthur (*pausing in his efforts*) I say! How frightfully embarrassin'. (*To the audience*) Is there any Sanatogen in the house? (*He has another attempt at lifting the sword, but gives up. To the Page*) You can have it back now.

The Page takes the sword and effortlessly holds it upright as before

(*Reacting*) Phew! I think I need a little rest! Have you finished with me, Guinie, old thing?
Guinevere For the moment!
Arthur I'll toddle off then. Toodle pip! (*He waves to the audience*) Toodle pip!

They call back

(*To Merlin*) I say! What a thoroughly nice shower!

Waving to the audience, he exits R, *followed by Merlin and the Page*

The Chorus exits

Guinevere (*to the audience*) There you are! That's what I've got to put with! 'E's about as much use as a glass 'ammer! (*To Olivia, indicating the bag*) Which do you think I should give to Lancelot?
Olivia Why not *all* of them, Your Majesty?
Guinevere 'Ere! Thas a good idea! That way 'e's bound to like one of 'em!
Olivia If I may speak boldly, Your Majesty. You seem especially fond of Sir Lancelot.
Guinevere Oh, I am, me dear! And when you meet 'im you'll know why. Oo! 'E's a real 'unk! Oh yes! 'E's Mel Gibson, Bruce Willis and Julian Clary all rolled into one! And 'andsome! Oh! 'E makes (*latest heart-throb*) look like (*latest ugly*)!
Olivia I have heard he is very brave and chivalrous.
Guinevere Well 'e certainly chivals my rous, I can tell ya that! Now run along and wrap those things up. 'E'll be 'ere in a minute.
Olivia (*curtsying*) Yes, Your Majesty.

She exits L *with the bag*

Guinevere (*to the audience*) Oh, I do wish I could afford to buy Lancelot a really expensive prezzy. But between you an' me an' the drawbridge, things are a bit tight 'ere in Camelot at the moment. Oh, I'll know you'll say I look like a million dollars — (*she waits for a response*) All right, don't take a vote on it! — But it's true! Things are so tight we've 'ad to go into the used armour business. We call ourselves "Rent a Dent"! Oh, I wish there was some way of makin' Camelot rich. My Arthur suggested somethin' called — a lottery! Whatever that is! As far as I can see it's all a load of balls and bits of paper! Well, per'aps we'll try it in the future if things get really tough. Until then, I must do as all good queens do!

Song 2

After, there is noise and excitement as the Chorus enter from the sides

Arthur rushes on from R, *followed by Merlin and the Page*

Arthur (*waving to the audience*) What ho! I say, Guinie, old thing! He's here! Good old Lancelot's here!

Excited, Guinevere preens herself. Merlin and the Page move to RC. *Arthur and Guinevere move to* LC, *and stand together*

Olivia enters from L, *with gift wrapped boxes and stands behind the queen. Merlin bangs his wand to call order*

Merlin   Prepare to greet Sir Lancelot, a knight without fear.
                    Let us welcome our hero with a good…
Arthur   Pint of beer! Haw! Haw! Haw!

Guinevere digs Arthur in the ribs to silence him

Merlin   Let us welcome our hero with a good rousing cheer!
Knight Three cheers for Sir Lancelot! Hip! Hip!
All Hurray!

Amid the cheers, handsome young Sir Lancelot enters on the raised walk. He pauses to wave to the ensemble, then comes down the steps to greet Arthur and Guinevere

Lancelot (*bowing grandly to Arthur*) Sire!

Guinevere eagerly presents her hand

   Your Majesty!

He kisses her hand

Guinevere (*aside to audience as he does so*) Oo! I can feel me toe nails curlin' up!

Arthur Welcome home, Lancelot. I trust the jolly old quest was successful.

Lancelot Indeed, sire. The invaders have all been routed. The good peasants of (*nearby town or village*) can once more sleep safely in their beds!

All Hurray!

Arthur Jolly good show! (*Preparing for a cosy chat*) Now, I want to hear all the gory details. How many invaders were there, and ——

Guinevere (*elbowing him aside*) Arthur! *I* wish to speak!

Arthur That'll make a nice change!

Guinevere (*gushing*) Welcome 'ome, *dear* Lancelot. Every night since you went away I've lain awake, 'opin you were safe and thinkin' about your predicaments. (*Aside to audience*) And, oh, what lovely predicaments! (*To Lancelot*) As a token of my afflictions, I would like you to except these welcome 'ome gifts. Lady Olivia — the prezzies!

Olivia (*coming forward*) Yes, Your Majesty.

She goes to Lancelot, and with a curtsy, presents the boxes to him. Their eyes meet and there is a pause

Guinevere (*elbowing Olivia out of the way*) I 'ope you like them, Lancelot. I chose 'em with me own fair 'and.

Lancelot Your Majesty is too kind. Thank you. I can't wait to open them.

Arthur (*aside to Lancelot*) I shouldn't hold your breath, old boy!

Sally (*off* L; *calling*) Yoo Hoo!

Sally rushes on from L *and pushes through the Chorus*

Where is 'e? Where is 'e? (*She searches about*) Come out, come out wherever you are! It's your little Sallywally! (*Not finding Squirt, she gets alarmed*) Where is 'e? (*Rushing to Lancelot*) Where is 'e? What 'ave you done with 'im?

Lancelot Who are you looking for, Sally?

Sally My Squirtykins!

Guinevere 'Er *what*?

Lancelot (*amused*) I think she means my squire, Squirt.

Sally nods eagerly

Well, he's around somewhere. I expect he's with his new friend.

Sally New friend?

Lancelot He's probably showing her the castle grounds.

Sally *Her*?

Lancelot Yes. We met her on our travels and brought her back with us. She and Squirt have become very fond of each other.
Sally (*now in utter despair*) Oh no! 'E's got a new girl friend! 'E doesn't love me anymore! *Waaah!*

Wailing at the top of her lungs, she blunders off L *through the Chorus*

Lancelot (*calling after her*) Sally, wait! Let me explain…
Guinevere Oh, save yer breath, Lancelot! One just can't get the staff these days!

Squirt enters backwards, talking to someone off DR

Squirt Now, come on. Don't be shy. No-one's goin' to hurt you. You trust Squirt, don't you? Yes. I'm taking you to meet the king and queen. You'll like King Arthur, he's a lovely chap. And Queen Guinevere looks just like a picture ——
Guinevere (*preening herself*) Oh!
Squirt — that hasn't developed properly!
Guinevere (*roaring*) *What*?
Squirt (*jumping and spinning around*) Ahh! (*To the audience*) Whoops! (*To Guinevere*) Sorry, Yer Maj! Only jokin'! How nice it is to see your royalships again! (*He does a comic bow*)
Guinevere Who've you got out there?
Squirt Someone you're just goin' to fall in love with! (*To the audience*) And so are you! Now, she's a bit shy, so don't make any noise or sudden movements.

He goes off R *and returns leading on Smoulder, a little dragon*

All react

Here she is! This is Smoulder, the dragon. Isn't she lovely?
Guinevere (*shrieking and hiding behind Arthur*) Ahh! It's a dragon! 'Elp! Save me! It's a great big 'orrible dragon!
Squirt Oh, she's not big and she's certainly not 'orrible (*To the audience*) Is she, kids? And she's got very good manners. Give the nice people a little wave, Smoulder.

Smoulder waves to the audience

There! (*To Guinevere*) See how polite she is.
Guinevere I don't care if she 'as tea with (*newsworthy or local personality*)! Keep it away from me!

Lancelot Your Majesty, Smoulder is quite harmless, I assure you.
Squirt Yes! Go on, Smoulder. Go and say hallo to the Royal Jellies.

He gives her a little push

Smoulder goes over to Arthur and Guinevere. They retreat, Guinevere still hiding behind Arthur. Smoulder holds out her paw to Arthur. Tentatively he takes it and gives it a shake

Arthur (*beaming as he does so*) Oh, I say! Haw! Haw! Haw! What an absolutely spiffin' little dragon!

Smoulder offers her paw out to Guinevere

Go on, Guinie, old thing! Give her paw a shake.
Guinevere Not without asbestos gloves! I'm not getting my fingers barbecued!
Lancelot Oh, she's far too young to start breathing fire yet, Your Majesty!
Squirt Yeah! That's why we call 'er Smoulder! Go on, she won't 'urt you.
Guinevere Oh, I dunno (*To the audience*) Shall I?

"Yes!" from the audience

D'you really think so?

"Yes!" from the audience

Are you sure?

"Yes!" from the audience

Oh, all right then!

Very tentatively she takes Smoulder's paw and shakes it; everyone cheers and applauds. Guinevere is now very proud of herself

Rolf Harris, eat yer 'eart out! Oh, she's not such a bad little scaly scallywag, after all!

She pats Smoulder on the head

Lancelot Your Majesties, we brought Smoulder back with us hoping you'd accept her as a royal pet.

Guinevere A royal pet? Well, I *was* thinkin' of gettin' myself a corgi, but
— no. A dragon'll be much better. And when she's old enough to start
breathin' fire, she'll save us pounds on our heatin' bill.

She shakes Smoulder's paw and pats her on the head

Welcome to Castle Camelot, little Smoulder! Consider yerself one of the
family!

Song 3

*A lively number involving everyone with perhaps a little dance solo for
Smoulder*

Guinevere (*to Squirt*) 'Ere! 'Angabout! What does a baby dragon eat?
Squirt Only one meal a day! A few lumps of coal, a box of matches and three
firelighters!

Smoulder rubs her belly

Come on, young Smoulder! Let's see if we can find you some. Wave
goodbye to everyone. Bye! Ta ta!

Waving to the ensemble and the audience, Squirt and Smoulder exit L

Guinevere It'll seem odd 'avin' a real live dragon livin' in Camelot Castle.
Arthur Not for me, old thing. I'm used to it! *You've* been livin' here for
years! Haw! Haw! Haw!

Guinevere is about to give him a swipe

A Servant enters from R, *and kneels before Arthur*

Servant Sire! Two persons have arrived at the castle and crave an audience
with you.
Arthur Who are they?
Servant Morgana and her son Mordred, sire. She says she is your majesty's
cousin.
Arthur By Jove! Cousin Morgana, eh! Well, fancy that! Ask her to come
in.
Servant Yes, sire.

The servant rises and exits R

Guinevere You didn't tell *me* you 'ad a cousin Banana, or whatever 'er name
  is!
Arthur I'd forgotten all about her. Haven't seen her since we were kiddies.
  Awfully strange girl. Used to like pullin' the wings off flies, I remember.

The others react with disgust

  Still, I expect she's got over that by now.
Merlin   *Sire*, of Morgana I have heard many sinister tales!
                        For years she has dwelt in the country of Wales!
Arthur Oh dash it all! You can't hold *that* against her! After all, *someone*
  has to live there!
Merlin   I hear she practises the art of sorcery!
                        Beware, in case she means you some treachery!
Guinevere Ugh! She sounds a real nasty piece of work!
Arthur Nonsense, old sausage! I bet she's a frightfully nice sort of person!

*Morgana sweeps on from R followed by scowling Mordred. Both are the
picture of evil incarnate!*

All react!

  (*Aside to Guinevere*) On the other hand, I might be wrong! (*To Morgana*)
  W... What ho, Morgana, old girl! Awfully nice to see you again — simply
  awful — welcome to my wart... I mean, my court.
Morgana (*with a mocking bow*) Cousin Arthur! (*Sneering*) Or should I say
  — King Arthur! Allow me to present my son, Mordred.
Mordred (*with a sneer*) Your Majesty.
Arthur What ho, Morbid... I mean...

Guinevere wanting to be introduced, gives him a nudge

  Oh, yes! This is Queen Guinevere. My little woman!
Morgana (*to Mordred*) Little? He needs his eyes testing!

They both snigger and Guinevere bristles

Guinevere (*very haughty*) My husband and I — 'ave been married for many
  years! Arthur fell in love with me the moment we met. 'E was blind with
  love!
Mordred (*to Morgana*) Blind *drunk* more like!

*They snigger again and Guinevere looks as if he's going to explode. Arthur
steps in, trying to keep the party sweet*

Arthur presents Merlin

Arthur And this is good old Merlin.

Morgana (*sneering*) Ah, yes. Merlin the *good* wizard. What a shame your talents have been wasted here in Camelot.

Merlin   My magical powers are at the service of my king. They are used only for good, not evil or suffering!

Morgana ⎱ (*together; to the audience*) Yuk! What a creep!
Mordred ⎰

Guinevere (*aside to Arthur*) 'Urry up 'an get rid of 'em! They're worse than (*popular nasty*)!

Arthur Well, Morgana, is this a social call, or ——

Morgana (*taking the floor*) Listen to me, all of you! And listen well! Many years ago my cousin Arthur pulled the sword from the stone and was made king. I was never given the chance! Huh! Girls and women were not allowed! I left the shores of Britain determined that one day I would return and challenge Arthur's right to the throne! That day has now come!

General sensation

Arthur (*unsettled, but trying to make light of it*) Haw! Haw! And how do you propose to do it, old fruit?

Morgana In a way that will appeal to your sickening sense of fair play, Arthur. I propose a tournament on the jousting field! A contest between your champion and my son Mordred! If your champion wins, Mordred and I will leave these shores and never return…

Arthur Good show!

Morgana But! If Mordred wins — you will step down from the throne and I shall rule in your place!

General sensation and uproar

Well, cousin? Do you accept my challenge?

Guinevere Don't do it, Arthur! Tell 'er to go an' sling 'er 'ook!

Arthur (*to Morgana*) This contest — it would have to be an absolutely fair fight. No magic or jiggery-pokery.

Morgana I give you my word that no magic will be used — (*to Merlin*) on *either* side! (*To Arthur*) The rules of the tournament I leave entirely up to you.

Arthur (*to Merlin*) What do you think, old bean?

Merlin   I view the matter with grave suspicion! But you are king! It is your decision.

Arthur Lancelot, how do you feel about fighting old Morbid over there?

Lancelot I would do it without hesitation, sire!

Arthur That settles it then! (*To Morgana, drawing himself up to full height*) Righto! I accept your jolly old challenge!

Chorus Hurray!

Guinevere (*groaning and slapping her forehead*) Oh, no!

Arthur The contest will take place this very afternoon on the Royal Jousting Field! And — (*he puts his arm around Lancelot's shoulder*) may the best man win!

Morgana (*putting her arm around Mordred's shoulder*) Oh, he will!

Arthur I don't think your little boy stands a chance against Lancelot. He's the best knight of the year! He's never been beaten.

Morgana We shall see! (*Aside to audience*) I have a plan to make sure he will be beaten *this* time! (*She gives her evil laugh*) Ha! Ha! Ha! (*To Arthur*) It is agreed then! Until this afternoon — farewell! Come, Mordred!

She sweeps our R followed by Mordred

Guinevere (*rounding on Arthur*) You regal twit! 'Ave you gone completely off yer royal rocker! What if that gruesome twosome win! We'll lose everythin'! Our crowns! The castle! Our front row tickets for (*local event/ football match; in utter misery*) We'll 'ave to join the workin' classes! (*Rounding on him again*) You'll 'ave to go out and find a job.

Arthur Oh crikey! I hadn't thought of that!

Lancelot Fear not, Your Majesties. I shall not fail you.

Guinevere You'd better not!

She stomps out L

Arthur (*calling after her*) Don't be like that, old thing!… (*To audience*) I bet (*topical personality*) doesn't have to put up with this! Toodle pip!

He waves, then runs out after Guinevere

(*As he goes*) Guinie, old thing…

Merlin and the Page follow him out

Olivia is about to go, but Lancelot stops her. Note: The Chorus can exit at this point if so desired

Lancelot (*to Olivia*) A moment, my lady. (*He bows*) You are new at Camelot.

Olivia Yes, Sir Knight. I have recently joined the court as lady-in-waiting to the queen.

Lancelot A lady-in-waiting, eh? Waiting for what, I wonder.
Olivia I do not understand you, Sir Knight.
Lancelot Oh, please dispense with the Sir Knight! Call me Lancelot. Or —
(*moves closer*) Lance would be much sweeter on the ear.
Olivia (*moving away a little*) Ought you not to be preparing for this
afternoon's contest?
Lancelot Ha! 'Twill be no contest. I assure you. I will beat that dolt in the
first round! (*Slight pause*) But there is *one* contest that is not so easily won.
Olivia Indeed?
Lancelot Ay. (*He moves closer*) The contest to win the heart of a beautiful
lady. (*He takes her hands*) A lady-in-waiting, perhaps.

Song 4

*A romantic duet, with romantic lighting. If the Chorus remain, they could
take up the singing as Lancelot and Olivia dance together*

A picture finish, and the Lights fade to Black-out

SCENE 2

Outside the castle walls

Tabs, or a front cloth showing the outer walls of Camelot

Sinister music and eerie lighting

Morgana and Mordred enter from DL. *They sneer at the audience*

Morgana (*pointing at the audience*) Look, Mordred, my son! Look at all
those puny, pathetic, putrid peasants! Once I am queen, they will all be my
slaves. Ha! Ha! Ha!
Mordred Yes Mummy! Especially those from (*local place or school*)! They
need taking down a peg or two!
Morgana *And* the ones from (*somewhere else*)! I shall enjoy making *their*
lives a misery! Ha! Ha!

*They sneer and provoke the audience for a little, then Mordred becomes
obviously troubled*

Mordred Er... Mummy?
Morgana What is it, my little soldier?
Mordred I... I'm a teensy weensy bit worried.

Morgana Why, my pet? Tell your mummy all about it.

Mordred (*nervously twisting up the end of his cloak*) Well — it's the jousting contest with Lancelot this afternoon. I… I've not been feeling quite myself since that bout of the Black Death, and — and my bad leg's playing me up again, and — and Lancelot's a much better fighter than I am, and — and (*a wail*) *I'm scared he'll beat me up!*

He sobs pitifully on Morgana's shoulder

Morgana (*comforting him*) There, there! Diddums. Don't cry.

He starts sucking the end of his cloak

It's all right, Mummy's here. (*Suddenly turning vicious, and slapping the cloak away from his mouth*) Don't *do* that! Stop showing me up in front of this rabble! Act your age!

Mordred regains control of himself

Better now?

He nods

You have nothing at all to worry about. Your mummy will see to everything. (*She looks about to make sure the coast is clear*) Listen. I have prepared a magic potion that Lancelot will drink before the tournament begins. It will make him tired, weak and useless! In that state he will be unable to defend himself and you can slaughter him without any difficulty!

Mordred (*overjoyed*) Oh, brilliant! (*Demonstrating*) I'll *hack* him to pieces! I'll *cut* him down to size! I'll *knock* his block off! I'll… (*a sudden thought*) But, Mummy! How are we going to get him to drink the potion?

Morgana Leave that to me! Mummy will find a way. I always do, because — (*to the audience*) I'm the best! Ha! Ha! Ha!

Mordred (*to the audience*) Oh, yes she is!

"Oh no she isn't! Oh, yes she is!" routine with audience

Then Morgana and Mordred exit DR

The lighting becomes brighter

Sally is heard wailing off DL

She runs on in floods of tears followed by Squirt

Squirt Sally! What's up?Why the water works? (*Going to her*) Sally, my little Sugar Plum!
Sally (*moving away from him*) Go away! I never want to see you again!
Squirt But what 'ave I done?
Sally (*turning on him*) You *know* what you've done! You're a two timin', double crossin', two faced *philanderer*!
Squirt A philanderer? But I don't know anything about stamps!
Sally You don't?

She stamps on his toe and he hops about in agony

There's one! Start a collection!
Squirt (*hobbling to her*) I wish I knew what I've done to upset you, Sally. All the time I was away on the quest I kept thinkin' about you. Every time we came up against somethin' really nasty an' 'orrible, I'd think of you.
Sally It didn't stop you finding a new girlfriend though, did it?
Squirt Eh? A new girlfriend? What are you talkin' about, Sally?
Sally Oh, don't play the innocent with me! I know all about it! Sir Lancelot told me! 'E said you brought her back to Camelot with you! (*Starting to blub*) 'E... 'E said you an' she were... very fond of each other! (*Wailing*) *You don't love me anymore*! (*She turns away and sobs against the proscenium,* L)
Squirt (*to the audience*) What's she goin' on about, kids? I 'aven't got a new girlfriend! Someone I brought back to Camelot? 'Ere! You don't think she means little Smoulder, do you? Yeah! That's it! Ha! Ha! Oh, we'll 'ave some fun with Sally now! Don't let on, will ya? (*He gives them a wink and saunters across to Sally*) Sally, I 'ave a confession to make. You're right. I *do* 'ave a new girlfriend!
Sally (*wailing*) Waaah!

Each time she wails, Squirt has to turn away to suppress his laughter

Squirt Yes. And she's ever so cute. (*To the audience, encouraging them*) Isn't she kids?

"Yes!" from the audience

Sally Waaah!
Squirt And she's a lot younger than you! (*To the audience*) Isn't she kids?

"Yes!" from the audience

Sally Waaah!
Squirt And she's a fantastic little mover! (*To the audience*) Isn't she, kids?

"Yes!" from the audience

Sally Waaah!
Squirt Oh, yes! She's a right little cracker! And one of these days she's really goin' to set the world on fire! (*To the audience*) Isn't she, kids?

"Yes!" from the audience

Sally Waaah!
Squirt Would you like to meet her?
Sally (*stamping her foot*) No!
Squirt Oh, thas a shame. 'Cos she'd love to meet you.
Sally (*storming at him*) Oh, you've got a nerve! Bringin' that 'ussy 'ere! Flountin' 'er in my face! (*She turns away*) Wos *she* got that I aven't got?
Squirt (*to the audience, sniggering*) A tail for one thing! (*To Sally*) Are you sure you don't want to meet 'er? She's just outside.
Sally No! Yes! I *will* meet 'er! Just to give 'er a piece of my mind.
Squirt Can you spare it?
Sally What?
Squirt I'll just go an' fetch 'er.

Unseen by Sally, he winks to the audience, exits R, *and returns with Smoulder*

He indicates to the audience to remain quiet

Sally (*with her back to them*) I'll teach 'er to steal *my* boyfriend! The trollop! She won't know what's 'it 'er! The Jezebel! I'll knock 'er into the middle of next week!
Squirt Sall. 'Ere she is!
Sally (*still with her back to them*) So! You're the tramp who stole my Squirty away, are you! Well, I've got just one thing to say to you… (*She turns*) Ahhh!
Squirt Sally, I'd like you to meet Smoulder. Smoulder, this is Sally.
Sally (*flabbergasted*) B-B-But, it's a— it's a…
Squirt A baby dragon. *She's* my new girlfriend.
Sally Then you mean — I'm still your only *girl* girlfriend?
Squirt Of course you are, Sally!
Sally (*over the moon*) Oh, my Squirtykins!

*She rushes across and hugs and squeezes Squirt. She then does the same to
Smoulder*

Squirt (*to someone in the audience*) Look out! You're next!
Sally I think Smoulder an' I are goin' to be great friends!
Squirt Yes, you'll be just like those two in the X files! — Smoulder and
Sally!

*He guffaws at his "joke". Sally groans, and Smoulder puts her paws over her
ears and shakes her head*

(*To the audience*) If you thought *that* was bad — get a load of this! (*To the
pianist or conductor*) Take it away, Sir Andrew!

Song 5

*A comedy song and dance for Squirt and Sally. Smoulder joins in with comic
capers*

To end, they all dance out DR, *waving to the audience as they go*

Guinevere, looking worried and anxious, enters from DL

Guinevere (*to the audience, gloomily*) 'Allo! Sorry I'm not my usual
skinfullatin' self, but I'm feelin' very agitated. In fact my agi 'as never been
so tated! I'm that worried about this joustin' contest! Suppose Lancelot
doesn't win and Morgana, the piranha, takes over! What'll it be like in
Camelot then? It'll be worse than livin' in (*local reference*)! Oh, that stupid
'usband of mine! Why did 'e 'ave to agree to it? But that's a man all over,
isn't it, girls? Take somethin' on and never mind the quenseconces! Oh, I
do wish there was some way of makin' sure Lancelot wins!

Morgana enters from DL. *She is disguised in a long tattered cloak with
hood, and carries a small tray with bottles, jars and a small glass phial*

Morgana (*as a frail old woman*) Good-day, young woman.
Guinevere (*looking about*) Young woman…? What young woman…?
Who's she… Oh, of course! She means *me*! (*To Morgana*) What can I do
for you? You very charmin' old woman with excellent eyesight.
Morgana I am a poor gypsy. I travel the highways and byways selling my
wares in order to buy a little bread to eat. You've got a kind face.
Guinevere (*to the audience*) And the first one who says "But we don't know
what kind!" gets a knuckle sandwich! (*To Morgana*) Go on.

Morgana Please buy something from me.
Guinevere Not today, thank you!

Guinevere moves to R *exit*

Morgana Wait, fair damsel!
Guinevere (*coming back*) You called? (*To the audience*) I'm always receptacle to flattery! (*To Morgana*) Yes?
Morgana I am sure I must have something that a lovely young maiden like you would desire. (*Offering a jar*) This perfume perhaps?

Guinevere takes the jar and sniffs it. She staggers back, coughing and spluttering

Guinevere Pooh! Cor! Talk about "Obsession"! That's more like *obstruction*! I want to *attract* men, not knock 'em out! (*Giving the jar back*) What else 'ave ya got?
Morgana (*offering another jar*) This cream. It removes all wrinkles.
Guinevere (*taking it*) All wrinkles, eh? From everywhere?

Morgana nods

Even those around the ——

She whispers to Morgana

Morgana Even those. (*After a glance at Guinevere's posterior*) But I would strongly advise you to purchase the large economy size.
Guinevere (*to the audience*) What a flippin' cheek! (*She thrusts the jar back*) What else?
Morgana (*holding up another jar*) This hair lotion. It will make your hair shine like the morning dews!
Guinevere Yes! And be bald as a coot by the evenin' news! No, ta! I'll stick with (*well known brand of shampoo with any advertising campaign that goes with it*)! Well, I don't think you've got anythin' that *I* need!

Guinevere starts for R *exit*

Morgana Wait! There is one more thing! (*She holds up a small glass phial*) This!
Guinevere (*coming back out and peering at it*) What's that? Ronnie Corbett's (*or small local personality*) milk bottle?

Morgana One drop of this potion in a goblet of wine and you will have the strength of ten men.

Guinevere What good is that to me? I don't want the strength of ten men! In case you 'adn't noticed — (*striking a pose*) I am a delicate, fragile female!

Morgana Surely you know of some gallant knight who could make use of it. One who is about to fight in a battle, or — a jousting contest?

Guinevere (*to the audience*) Of course! *Lancelot*! (*To Morgana*) And a drop of that jollop would give 'im the strength of ten men?

Morgana Indeed! He who drinks of this potion will become invincible! (*Sports person*) swears by it!

Guinevere Then I'll 'ave it! 'Ow much?

Morgana A pound.

Guinevere Just a minute while I go to the cash point! (*Comic contortions as she hunts for the money up her knicker leg*) It's 'ere somewhere! I seem to be 'aving a cash flow problem! *Ah*! No! The pound's dropped again! (*More wriggling about, and there is a loud ripping noise: Velcro*) Oh 'eck! That's torn it! You wouldn't settle for 'alf a knicker, would ya? *Ah*! 'Ere it is. (*She produces a coin*) Phew!

She gives the money to Morgana and takes the phial

(*To the audience*) I'll get Lancelot to drink this before the contest, and 'e's bound to win!

Very pleased with herself, Guinevere skips out DR

Morgana throws back her hood and laughs her evil laugh

The stage grows dark. Morgana is lit by an eerie spotlight

Morgana Ha! Ha! Ha! Ha! Little does she realize that the potion will make Lancelot totally useless! Mordred will make mincemeat of him, and then — the throne will be mine! *All mine*! Ha! Ha! Ha! Ha!

Laughing her evil laugh, she sweeps out DL, *amid boos and hisses*

The Lights fade to Black-out

SCENE 3

The Joust Tournament

Sky blue cyclorama with hedge ground row. UC *is the "Royal Box" with its red and gold awning, crown motifs, banners and shields, etc. A bell is attached to the right side of the box. On each side of the stage is a small striped tent with practical openings. Red and white stripes on* R, *black and white stripes on* L. *A small stool is set below each tent*

There is a fanfare, and the scene is revealed

The chorus are discovered, eagerly awaiting the joust. A few Vendors and Street Entertainers mingle with the crowd. They all sing

A fanfare

The chorus move quickly to the sides. Grand processional music is played

The dancers, as heralds carrying standards, enter and march around the stage. The march changes into a dance routine

Song 6

After, the dancers can exit, or remain at the sides, holding up their standards

Merlin enters and moves C. *He bangs his wand*

Merlin   Show due reverence to those who draw near.
                    Pay homage to King Arthur and Queen Guinevere!

Merlin moves to RC

A fanfare

All bow and curtsy

Arthur and Guinevere enter, followed by the Page, carrying Excalibur, and Olivia carrying a goblet and a red scarf. They move to C

Arthur (*greeting the gathering*) What ho, my jolly old objects! Haw! Haw! Haw! (*He spots the audience and points them out to Guinevere*) Look, Guinie, old thing! The (*local*) mob are still here! (*Waving to the audience*) What ho!

Guinevere (*at her regal best*) My husband and I wish to welcome you all to the Camelot Community Leisure Centre and Jousting Field!

Arthur Absolutely! Now you all know why we're here. There's an awful lot ridin' on this fight. Namely, my jolly old crown and whatnot! So, let's hope that ——

Guinevere (*nudging him*) Oh, get on with it!

Arthur Er… yes! So, without further ado, I'll hand you over to your Master of Ceremonies for the afternoon — good old Merlin! (*He leads the applause*)

Everyone claps, then Merlin takes a bow, and bangs his wand

Merlin (*a la boxing MC*)   Ladies and Gentlemen!
In the Red Corner! The reigning champion of Camelot!
Your own! Your very own! Sir Lancelot!

All cheer, as Lancelot enters from his tent R. He wears stylized red armour and carries his helmet. He acknowledges the crowd

Squirt, Sally and Smoulder rush from his tent, waving red pom-poms. They perform a cheer leader type routine across the front

Squirt }
Sally }   Lancelot, Lancelot! Ra! Ra! Ra!
Smoulder }   Lancelot, Lancelot! Ya! Ya! Ya!
Lancelot, Lancelot! Knock him down!
Lancelot, Lancelot! Save the crown!
Lancelot, Lancelot! Blow him away!
Lancelot, Lancelot! Will win today!
Lancelot!

All cheer

The three clear to R. Merlin bangs his wand

Merlin   In the black corner!
The man who opposes our royal throne!
Greet Mordred!
With suitable boo and groan!

All boo and hiss, as Mordred enters from his tent L. He wears stylized black armour and carries his helmet. Morgana follows him out, carrying a black scarf

Merlin bangs his wand

The rules of the Joust I will now relate.
The best of three rounds shall decide our fate.
The first — on horseback with lance and shield!
The second — on foot with battleaxe to wield!
The third and final— with trusty sword!
(*Aside*) That's if Mordred hasn't already been floored!
(*Aloud*) Now, by tradition and ancient lore,
Favours may be given to each competitor!

Morgana ties the black scarf around Mordred's arm

All boo

Guinevere takes the red scarf from Olivia, and ties it around Lancelot's arm

All cheer

Guinevere There's somethin' else I'd like to give Lancelot before we start
the punch up! (*She takes the goblet from Olivia*) I'd like 'im to drink my
'ealth from this gobin of wine.
Morgana Well, *I* have no objections to that. Have you, Mordred?
Mordred None at all.

They exchange knowing looks

Arthur Well, I jolly well have! Guinie, old thing! We can't allow drinkin'
before the fight, y'know! It's simply not on!
Guinevere But ——
Arthur (*very sternly for him*) Guinevere! King Hubby has spoken! No
drinking before the fight!

*Guinevere is gobsmacked. Unseen by the others, Mordred is shaken by the
news and Morgana has to calm him down*

(*To Merlin*) Righto! Let's get this jolly old show on the road!
Merlin   Contestants, 'tis time to pit your forces!
                          Away with you now, and mount your horses!

Lancelot bows and exits above his tent

Mordred tries to make a run for it DS, *but Morgana grabs him and pushes
him off above his tent, then turns to Arthur*

Morgana Cousin! Before the Joust begins, do I still have your solemn promise that you will relinquish the throne the moment Mordred wins?

Arthur (*on his dignity*) *I never* go back on my word, old fruit! Honour and chivalry and all that lot, what! Besides — haw! haw! — your little boy isn't goin' to win, is he?

Morgana Oh, yes he is!

"Oh, no he isn't!" "Oh yes, he is!" routine with Chorus and audience

Guinevere (*to audience, confidentially*) Lancelot will win for sure when I give 'im this potion! Won't 'e kids?

"No" from the audience

Eh? What's that?

But before they can enlighten her, Merlin comes forward and bangs his wand for silence

Merlin   All spectators must now retire!
                          Clear this field for things most dire!

He ushers them us. *Arthur, Guinevere, Olivia, the Page and Morgana enter the "Royal Box". Merlin remains outside, standing to the right of the box. When all are in position, he gives three solemn bangs of his wand*

A fanfare

> *From their respective sides, Lancelot and Mordred enter on "horseback" (see production notes). Both wear their helmets and carry modified shields and lances. They are greeted with cheers and boos*

Merlin bangs his wand for silence

> Lancelot and Mordred, before you do battle,
> Attend the king, and hark to his prattle!

Lancelot and Mordred rein their "horses" to face the box

Arthur (*to them*) Now then, you chaps. We want a good clean fight. No bashin' below the bread basket, or clobberin' close to the codpiece! Righto! Let battle commence!

Lancelot and Mordred back up their "horses", face each other and lower their lances

Merlin Round one! (*He rings the bell*)

Suitable music and roars from the crowd. Lancelot and Mordred charge at each other. After a couple of passes Mordred's lance is knocked to the ground

The music stops

All cheer

Merlin rings the bell

Merlin   Mordred's lance is on the ground!
                        Lancelot has won the first round!

All cheer

> *Lancelot and Mordred "ride" off above their tents. The fallen lance is removed*

> *Lancelot and Mordred enter from their tents and sit on the stools. (Note: if more time is required for them to "dismount", Squirt, Sally and Smoulder could repeat the cheerleader routine)*

Morgana rushes down to console Mordred. Guinevere goes to Lancelot with the goblet. The others chat quietly amongst themselves

> *Squirt exits into the tent* R

Guinevere Well done, Lancelot. That was a right belter!
Lancelot (*rising and bowing*) Thank you, Your Majesty!
Guinevere I bet you're feelin' proper parched after that. 'Ow about a nice drop of wine?

She offers the goblet

Lancelot (*taking it*) Thank you, Your Majesty.

Guinevere, Morgana and Mordred watch him with eager anticipation

(*He raises the goblet to his lips, then lowers it*) But the king said ——
Guinevere Oh, never mind 'im! Go on! 'Ave a good guzzle!
Lancelot Thank you. I will!

He is about to drink, when Arthur spots him and calls from the box

Arthur *Lancelot*! Stop that! I thought I told you, Guinie! No drinking! Take
it away, and come back here at once! Round two is about to start!

Lancelot hands back the goblet

*Guinevere stamps her foot in annoyance and stomps back to the box.
Morgana has to console the agitated Mordred*

  Squirt comes out of the tent carrying a battleaxe

*He gives it to Lancelot, who does a few practice swings with it. This terrifies
Mordred, and he tries to make a run for it. Morgana grabs him. She reaches
into his tent and brings out a battleaxe. She thrusts it into his hands, and
returns to the box*

Merlin Round two! (*He rings the bell*)

*Suitable music and roars from the crowd. Lancelot and Mordred circle each
other. After a couple of swings with their axes, Mordred points at the sky.
Lancelot looks up and Mordred pushes him over, causing his axe to fall to
the ground*

Boos from the crowd

Morgana cheers as Mordred struts about holding up his axe in triumph

Merlin rings the bell

            Lancelot's axe is on the ground!
            Mordred has won the second round!

All boo

*The axes are removed. Lancelot and Mordred sit on their stools. Morgana
rushes down to Mordred. Guinevere comes down to Lancelot with the goblet.
The others chat quietly as before*

  Squirt exits into his tent R

Lancelot (*to Guinevere, shamefaced*) I'm very sorry, Your Majesty.
Guinevere Never mind, Lancelot. I'm sure it was a dirty foul anyway! Still another round to go. (*After a quick glance in Arthur's direction*) Per'aps you'd like the little drinkie now, eh?

Guinevere offers Lancelot the goblet

Morgana and Mordred are watching, eagerly. Unseen, Arthur leaves the box and creeps up behind Guinevere

Lancelot No, thank you. You heard what his majesty said. He doesn't approve of drinking.
Guinevere Huh! Not much! You should see 'im down the (*local pub or club*) on Saturday night! Go on, just a little sip.

She offers Lancelot the goblet

Arthur (*stepping out*) Guinie!

She jumps with fright

You're at it again! How many times must I tell you? No drinking!
Guinevere Oh, but, Arthur! It's such a shame! It'll go flat!
Arthur Flat, eh? Well, if that's all you're worried about — I'll jolly well drink it myself!

He grabs the goblet and drinks

Guinevere
Morgana } (*together, to the audience*) Oh, no!
Mordred
Arthur (*handing back the goblet and smacking his lips*) Not a bad little wine! Very subtle. (*To Guinevere*) Now, come one, old thing. Back to our box, the... (*he starts to feel drowsy*) the final round is about to... (*yawn*) start. Good luck, Lancelot, old... (*yawn*) chap!

Yawning, he turns and literally drags himself back to the box

Gobsmacked, Guinevere watches him go. Morgana has to now cope with a very agitated Mordred

Guinevere (*to the audience*) The strength of ten *men*, eh? 'E hasn't got the strength of ten *butterflies*! There's somethin' funny goin' on 'ere — an' it ain't the jokes!

She goes back to the box

During the following action, Arthur falls asleep on Guinevere's shoulder, and she has to keep propping him up

Squirt comes out of the tent carrying a sword

He gives it to Lancelot, who does a few practice jabs with it. Seeing this, Mordred tries to make a run for it as before. Morgana grabs him. She reaches into his tent and brings out a sword. Thrusting it into his hands, she goes back to the box

Merlin Round three! (*He rings the bell*)

Suitable music and roars from the crowd. Lancelot and Mordred fight it out with the swords. It is not long before Mordred's sword is knocked to the ground

Great cheers

Merlin rings the bell

> Mordred's sword is on the ground!
> Lancelot has won the final round!

More cheering

Lancelot removes his helmet, and holds his sword aloft. Morgana rushes down to Mordred, not looking very pleased to say the least

Mordred (*holding out his arms, hoping to be comforted by her*) Mummy!
Morgana (*snarling at him*) Oh, shut up!
Merlin   In combat, Lancelot has won the day!
                     Good King Arthur must now have his say!

All turn and look towards Arthur. He is fast asleep on Guinevere's shoulder and snoring loudly

General reaction. Some giggling

Guinevere (*out of the corner of her mouth*) Arthur! Wake up! People are
  lookin'! *Wake up!*

She gives him a nudge and he slides down out of sight. Nonplussed Guinevere just smiles sweetly and gives the royal wave

Lancelot (*to all, taking charge*) As King Arthur, our rightful sovereign, is… er… indisposed. I shall speak on his behalf. Morgana. I have won the contest fairly. *You* must now abide by your part of the bargain! You and Mordred will leave Britain and never return!

All Ay!

Morgana (*snarling at them*) So be it! We will leave!

All Good!

Morgana (*aside to audience*) But not just yet! Ha! Ha! Ha! (*Aloud*) Come, Mordred!

Amid jeers and boos, she sweeps out L

Mordred dithers. Lancelot takes a step towards him, and he scuttles out after his mother

All laugh

Squirt Three cheers for Sir Lancelot! Hip! Hip!

All Hurray!

After the last cheer, Arthur emerges over the front of the box. His crown is askew

Arthur I say! What's goin' on? Did we win?

Lancelot Yes, sire!

Arthur Oh, jolly good show! Haw! Haw! Haw!

He comes out of the box, followed by the others, and shakes hands with Lancelot

Well done, old bean, well done! (*He looks about*) And what about the diabolical duo?

Lancelot Sent packing, sire!

Arthur Oh, spiffin'! Wish I'd seen that! (*He adjusts his crown*) Phew! Can't understand what happened to me, y'know. Must have been that wine of yours, Guinie! Jolly good job Lancelot didn't drink it, what?

Guinevere (*flustered and eager to get off the subject*) Er… yes! Er… Arthur, I think we should celebrate!

Arthur What an absolutely rippin' idea! I know! Let's all go on a picnic right now, and — and have a slap up banquet tonight! Everyone invited, of course!

All Hurray!

Song 7

A jolly song and dance involving all those on stage. To end, Lancelot is hoisted onto the shoulders of some of the men and paraded around

The Lights fade to Black-out

Scene 4

Outside the Castle Walls

Tabs, or the front cloth used in Act I, Scene 2

Sinister music and eerie lighting

Morgana and Mordred enter from DL

They are greeted by the usual barrage of abuse from the audience. Mordred is sulky and does not react. After a little solo by-play with the audience, Morgana turns on him

Morgana Oh, what's the matter with you, Mordred? You've got a face like (*local place*) on a wet weekend!
Mordred (*pouting*) I'm feeling sad, Mummy.
Morgana Why, my little sugar puff?
Mordred Because we're leaving. Just as I was getting so fond of our crumbly old castle with its creepy crypt and spooky spires. And all the rats and spiders in the dungeon. I've just made friends with each of them, and now we've got to leave!

Mordred starts to blubber

Morgana Now, don't upset yourself again, Mordred. Do you really think I meant what I said? Of course we're not leaving. Oh no! Your mummy isn't beaten yet! And from now on it's no more Mrs Nice Guy! King Arthur of Camelot is going to die!
Mordred When?
Morgana As soon as I've killed him! Ha! Ha! Ha!
Mordred Killed him! But how? He's got Merlin's magic and a castle full of loyal knights to protect him.

Morgana Exactly! We will get one of those loyal knights to do the killing for us! Someone who is always at Arthur's side. Someone he trusts with his life. Someone like — Lancelot!

Mordred Oh, yes! So we just go up to Lancelot and say: Hallo Lancelot! How about killing King Arthur for us!

Morgana You stupid boy! Listen. I will cast a spell on Lancelot. Once he is under its influence I can get him to do my bidding at any time. He will dispose of Arthur for us, and get himself executed for the crime! Thus, we will be killing two birds with one stone! Then I can seize the throne and become queen! Ha! Ha! Ha!

Mordred It's a good plan, Mummy. But how are you going to put the spell on Lancelot?

Morgana At this very moment he is on a picnic in the forest near our castle. We must go there at once. Get him on his own, and I will — (*with gestures*) weave my magic wiles on him! Ha! Ha! Ha!

Mordred Oh, you're so clever, Mummy! (*To the audience*) Isn't she clever?

"No!" from the audience

Morgana Oh, yes I am!

"Oh no you're not!" "Oh yes I am!" routine with the audience

(*Finally*) Come, Mordred! Let us not waste any more time with this *riff raff*!

They exit DR *amid boos and hisses*

The lighting becomes brighter

Smoulder scampers on from DL *to* C. *She waves to the audience*

Squirt ⎫
Sally ⎭ (*together; off* L, *calling*) Smoulder! Where are you? Smoulder!

Smoulder scampers off DR

A slight pause, and Squirt and Sally run on from DL

Squirt (*seeing the place is empty*) Oh! I'm sure she came this way! (*Calling*) Smoulder!

Sally Squirty, if we don't get to the picnic soon all the food'll be gone!

Squirt And if we don't find the queen's new pet soon, we'll *be* the picnic!

Sally Oh, Squirty! I'm ever so 'ungry! I'm so 'ungry, I could even eat a dinner at (*local school or café*)!

Squirt Oh, you're *always* 'ungry, Sall! You'd eat me, given 'alf a chance!

Sally (*getting amorous*) *Oo, I* would! With or without dressin'.

She cuddles up to him

Squirt Ger off! People are lookin'!

Sally I don't care! I love you, Squirtykins!

Squirt (*disentangling himself*) Not 'ere! The /Mr/Mrs/Miss (*local institute or personality known to be in the audience*) is watchin'!

Sally (*moving away in a sulk*) You don't love me anymore!

Squirt (*wearily*) Yes, I do!

Sally You don't like me at all!

Squirt Yes, I do!

Sally You don't want to see me again!

Squirt Yes, I do!

Sally You think I'm plain an' ugly!

Squirt Yes, I do!

Sally (*wailing*) Waaah!

Squirt I mean, no I don't!

Sally (*self-pitying*) It's because I'm a *menial*, isn't it?

Squirt I don't care what religion you are.

Sally It's because I'm just a poor kitchen maid! Doin' the washin' up. An' fillin' the pepper pots!

Squirt Yes, but you're the only Spice Girl for me!

Sally Do you mean it?

She rushes to him and hugs him very tightly

Oh, my Squirtykins!

Squirt (*hardly able to breathe*) You've got more than enough "Girl Power" for me!

Sally (*releasing him*) I'm still 'ungry though! Oh, let's go to the picnic, Squirty!

Squirt Not until we've found Smoulder. Oh, where is that little scaly scamp? (*Calling*) Smoulder! Where are you?

Sally Per'aps the boys and girls 'ave seen 'er, Squirty.

Squirt (*to the audience*) Hey, kids! Have you seen that little dragon?

The audience answer "Yes!"

Was she 'ere?

The audience answer "Yes!"

Well, if you see 'er again, give us a shout. Will you do that? Great! Thanks!

During the following, Smoulder enters from DR *and creeps up behind Squirt and Sally. The audience will be shouting "She's behind you!, etc. etc.*

Sally Because as soon as we find 'er, we can go to the picnic and get stuck into those lovely sandwiches ——
Squirt And cakes!
Sally An' ice-creams!
Squirt And jellies! And… what's that? Can you see her? Where is she?

"Behind you!" From the audience

Sally Behind us? Are you sure?
Squirt (*to Sally*) Let's look!

Business with them slowly turning and Smoulder keeping behind them. "Oh no, she isn't, etc., etc." This is repeated a few times. Eventually, they see Smoulder

Smoulder scampers off DR. *Squirt and Sally chase off after her, yelling "Smoulder! You come back 'ere! Smoulder!, etc."*

The Lights fade to Black-out

SCENE 5

The Enchanted Forest

Forest backcloth, ground row and side wings. There is a tree stump mid stage. The forest has a strange, magical and slightly sinister quality about it

Discovered: Arthur and Guinevere are sitting on a large hamper, RC. *He is fast asleep, and she is eating a chicken drumstick. On the ground, in front of them, is a table-cloth with the remains of a sumptuous picnic. Merlin and the Page are standing behind the hamper. Olivia is seated on the tree stump, with Lancelot sitting on the ground beside her. The Chorus are grouped about, holding goblets and plates. The Dancers or Children are performing a dance as the Chorus sing*

Song 8

After the number, the Dancers or Children gather before the Royals and bow. Guinevere, holding the drumstick between her teeth, applauds them. She gives the sleeping Arthur a nudge, and he falls off the hamper

Arthur (*sitting up, dazed*) I say! Who moved the drawbridge? (*He realizes where he is*) Oh! (*He sees the audience and waves to them*) What ho!

The audience call back. Arthur gets to his feet

I was having an awfully nice dream...
Guinevere (*barking at him*) Arthur!
Arthur (*flinching*) Which has turned into a nightmare! (*To Guinevere*) You barked, old thing?
Guinevere (*indicating the Dancers or Children*) The peasants 'ave just pirouetted in front of you!
Arthur Have they? The dirty beasts! Well, never mind. There's no proper facilities in the forest, is there, what? Haw! Haw! Haw!

Guinevere dismisses the Dancers or Children and they exit or join the Chorus

She finishes the drumstick and tosses it over her shoulder, making Merlin and the Page duck

Guinevere Well, that's all the grub gone! (*She rises*) What shall we do now? Got any suggestions, Merlin?
Arthur (*to Merlin*) Go on, old fruit! Be suggestive.
Merlin (*coming forward, full of foreboding*)
           Your Majesties, I hate to be a party pooper,
           But this forest after dark is *not* so super!
           When daylight fades, evil forces abound!
           This place becomes Hell's merry-go-round!
           When the powers of darkness materialize,
           To linger here would be most unwise.
Guinevere (*to the audience*) Right little Judith Chalmers, isn't 'e? 'E'd never get a job with *Wish You Were Here* (*or local travel agent*)!
Arthur Haw! Haw! If I didn't know better, Merlin, I'd say you'd been spending too much time with my creepy cousin Morgana.
Merlin   'Tis *her* evil presence that inhabits this place!
           Morgana is a danger to the whole human race!
Arthur Well, you needn't worry about her! She's jolly well packed her bags and gone!

Merlin   Sire, I may be old, but my brain isn't rusted!
                    Beware of that woman! She's not to be trusted!
                    Her ruined castle lies not far away!
                    Let us return to Camelot without delay!
Guinevere I think 'e's right, Arthur. This place *is* a bit spooky! It reminds
me of the (*local night-spot*) at chuckin' out time! (*To the Chorus*) Right!
We're goin'! Pack everythin' in the hampster!

During the following the Chorus put the table-cloth, mugs, plates, etc. into
the hamper

Besides, I need to go and titivate meself for tonight's banquet. You want
me to be stunnin' don't you? (*She pushes out her chest*)
Arthur I'm sure you'll be an absolute *knock out*, old thing!

Smoulder scampers on from L

Guinevere   Smoulder! There you are! (*She pats Smoulder's head*) I
wondered what 'ad 'appened to you! Well, you missed the picnic, I'm
afraid. Aah!

She gets the audience to "Aah!" with her

But, I did manage to save you somethin' from the barbecue!

Smoulder eagerly sits up and begs

'Ere it is! (*She takes out a piece of charcoal*) A lovely bit of charcoal!

She gives it to Smoulder

There! Now, don't eat it all at once, or you'll get 'eartburn!

Olivia comes forward with Lancelot

Olivia Hallo, Smoulder. Where's Squirt and Sally?

Smoulder points off L

In the forest?

Smoulder nods

Why are they still there?

Smoulder turns round in a circle a couple of times

You mean — they're lost?

Smoulder nods

Guinevere Oh, trust that pair of gormless twits! Now we'll 'ave to 'ang about waitin' for 'em!
Lancelot It's all right, Your Majesty. You all go back to Camelot. I'll stay here and wait for them.
Olivia Are you sure? You heard what Merlin said about this forest after dark.
Lancelot Don't worry about me. Remember — (*he strikes a heroic pose*) I am Sir Lancelot!

He laughs, and takes her hands

I shall be quite safe.
Olivia (*gazing lovingly into his eyes*) Oh, I do hope so.

Lancelot kisses her hand

Guinevere (*to the audience*) Well, bust me buttress an' ruin me ramparts! She didn't waste much time, did she, girls?

She exits R followed by Smoulder, Merlin, the Page and the Chorus, carrying the hamper. Olivia leaves Lancelot and runs after them

Arthur (*to Lancelot, indicating Olivia*) And jolly nice too, Lancelot! Well, see you back at Camelot, old bean! Toodle pip! (*To the audience*) Toodle pip!

The audience call back

Arthur exits R

Lancelot goes up and sits on the tree stump

Morgana and Mordred enter at the back and creep up behind him

The audience will be shouting warnings, but Lancelot appears to have gone deaf! Just as they are nearly upon him, voices are heard off L

Squirt ⎫ (*together; off* L, *calling*) 'Allo! Is there anybody there? 'Allo!
Sally ⎭

On hearing this Lancelot jumps up and moves to L. *Morgana and Mordred shrink back*

Lancelot (*calling off to* L) Squirt! Sally! This way! Over here!

Morgana and Mordred exit quickly at the back

Sally and Squirt enter from L

Squirt Cor! Are we glad to see you, Lancelot! We've been lost in that forest for ages! It was so dark in there, Sally an' I kept bumpin' into each other!
Sally (*cuddling up to him*) I enjoyed that bit!
Squirt We were tryin' to find little Smoulder. 'Ave you seen 'er?
Lancelot Yes. She's gone back to Camelot with the others.
Sally Gone back? Does that mean we've missed the picnic?
Lancelot I'm afraid so.
Sally (*stamping her foot*) Oh pooh! An' I was so lookin' forward to all that lovely food! (*Rounding on Squirt*) This is all your fault! I should 'ave been at the picnic 'ours ago, instead of playin' (*current endurance TV programme*) with you in the forest!
Lancelot Don't fret, Sally. I've saved you both something to eat.

He goes up, takes a basket from behind the tree stump, and gives it to Sally

Sally (*squealing with delight*) Ooo! Lovely yummy cakes! Are they Mr Kiplin's?
Squirt I don't care as long as they're not — wait for it! — *Rudy'ard*!

Squirt guffaws at his joke

Lancelot and Sally groan to the audience

Sally Come on! Let's sit down an' eat 'em!

Lancelot and Squirt take a cake each. Sally sits on the tree stump. The other two sit on the ground, facing front. All start eating

A huge, hideous hairy Spider descends slowly from directly above the tree stump

The audience will be shouting, but all three are too immersed in their cakes to notice. The Spider touches Sally's head. She pauses in mid munch. The Spider ascends a little. Sally shrugs and continues eating. The Spider descends again, and touches her head

> *This time Sally sees it, gives an enormous "Silent" scream, and runs out L, clutching the basket*

> *The Spider ascends out of sight*

Squirt Mmm! Cor! These cakes are smashin'! Aren't they, Sally? (*He turns and sees the empty stump*) Sal? Hey! Where is she?
Lancelot (*being diplomatic*) I expect she's gone to powder her nose.
Squirt (*dumbly*) Powder 'er wot?
Lancelot You know — spend a penny.
Squirt But there's no shops in the forest! (*Great dawning*) Oh! *That* sort of penny! Well, I might as well sit on the stump 'til she gets back.

He sits on the tree stump and eats his cake

> *The Spider descends. Repeat the business as before*

> *Squirt gives a "silent" scream, and runs out L*

> *The Spider ascends out of sight*

Lancelot (*finishing his cake*) That was delicious! I think I'll have another one. (*He stands and sees the empty stump*) Well! They've both disappeared now! It must be the cold weather! Come to think of it. (*He shivers*) It has got very cold all of a sudden. (*He sits on the tree stump*)

The lighting starts to dim

I hope those two won't be long. It's starting to get dark.

The lighting becomes eerie and strange. Ground mist swirls in from the sides. Suitable unearthly sounds and music are heard

> *The Dancers, as grotesque Demons, Sprites and Goblins, enter, as if from out of the mist and shadows*

They encircle Lancelot and perform a strange and hypnotic dance around him. He remains seated, totally mesmerized. Gradually, his eyelids droop, his head nods and he falls asleep. The Dancers retreat to the sides

Morgana and Mordred enter in a green spot and come forward to gloat

Morgana Ha! Ha! Ha! So! The great Sir Lancelot is now in my power!

*She goes to the sleeping knight and makes strange magical passes over him.
Then, she leans forward and speaks into Lancelot's ear, in a low, bewitching
voice*

Lancelot? Lancelot? Do you hear me?
Lancelot (*in a hypnotic voice*) I hear you.
Morgana I am your master.
Lancelot You are my master.
Morgana You will obey my voice at all times. Whatever my voice
commands, you will do it without fail.
Lancelot I will obey.

Morgana moves away, laughing her laugh of evil triumph

Morgana Ha! Ha! Ha! Ha! The fool is now under my control! Tonight he
will kill Arthur, and the throne shall be mine! Ha! Ha! Ha!

She goes back to Lancelot and speaks to him as before

Lancelot? Do you hear me?
Lancelot I hear you.
Morgana You will awake now and remember nothing of what has passed!
(*She makes magic passes over him*) Awake Lancelot!

Lancelot slowly starts to wake up

Morgana, Mordred and the Dancers exit, quickly

The lighting returns to normal and the sounds and music fade out

Lancelot (*yawning and stretching*) Oh! I... I seemed to have dozed off for
a minute. (*He stands up*) Now where are those two! (*He calls*) Squirt!
Sally!

Squirt and Sally enter timidly from L

Squirt H-has it gone, Lancelot?
Lancelot Has *what* gone?
Sally That great big 'airy spider!

Lancelot I haven't seen a spider. I haven't seen anything. Come on, you two!
Let's get back to Camelot. We don't want to be late for the banquet.
Sally Oh, yes! The banquet! All that lovely grub! Oh, I'm so 'ungry, I could
eat a horse! Couldn't you, Squirty?
Squirt (*doing impression of a horse*) *Naaaay!*

He guffaws and Sally pushes him out R. *Laughing, Lancelot follows them
out*

*There is a flash of lightning and a great roll of thunder. The eerie lighting and
ground mist returns*

*Morgana sweeps on, followed by Mordred and the Demons, etc. She stands
on the tree stump and raises her arms*

*There is another flash of lightning and roll of thunder. Morgana gives her evil
laugh*

Morgana Ha! Ha! Ha! Ha!
Tonight King Arthur will die for sure!
His reign of chivalry will be no more!
He'll die at the hands of his friend Lancelot!
And I shall be ruler of all Camelot!
Ha! Ha! Ha!

Song 9

*This can be an "evil" duet for Morgana and Mordred, backed by the Dancers
in a suitable routine (or) a wild, devilish display for the Dancers only,
watched by the gloating pair. Whatever is chosen, it must end with a terrifying
tableau of evil abandonment, as* ——

– The CURTAIN *falls*

ACT II

SCENE 1

The Banqueting Hall of Camelot

Castle backcloth and side wings showing the Great Hall decorated with weapons, shields, flags and banners, etc. UC, on a raised dais, are two thrones side by side

The CURTAIN *rises on a scene of raucous merriment. Arthur and Guinevere are seated on the thrones. He is rather tipsy, and conducts the proceedings with a large goblet of wine. Guinevere is watching his antics with stern disapproval. Merlin, looking rather bored, is standing on their right. Next to him is the Page, leaning on Excalibur and eating an apple. Lancelot, Olivia and the Chorus are* C, *singing the rousing opening song*

They move quickly to the sides as the Dancers run on and perform as court tumblers

Song 10

All cheer and applaud the Dancers as they bow and run off

Arthur rises, rather unsteadily, to his feet

Arthur Jolly good show! Haw! Haw! Haw! Frightfully well done! (*He spots the audience*) I say! Look! All our friends have come back! (*He totters forward and greets the audience*) What ho!

The audience call back

How absolutely spiffin' to see you again! (*He peers out and has difficulty focusing*) Funny! There seems to be a lot more of you! *Double*, in fact! We've been having a super-duper time here at the jolly old banquet. Lashings of lovely food, and (*he holds up his goblet*) whatnot! Cheers! (*He drinks*)

Guinevere (*storming down and barking at him*) Arthur!

Arthur (*coughing and spluttering*) Oh! Uuugh! I say, don't *do* that, old thing! It upsets a chap's plumbin', don't y'know!

Guinevere What d'you think you're playin' at! Everyone's lookin'! Stop makin' an expedition of yerself!

Arthur (*to the audience*) You've met the little wife, haven't you? My Queenie! (*He puts his arm around her*) My little Guinie Winnie! I don't know what I'd do without her! I'd have a lot of fun trying, though! Haw! Haw! Haw! No, *no*! Must be fair! She's a wonderful woman! Very big hearted! In fact, she's very big in all directions! Haw! Haw! Haw! And she's got all dressed up for the evening as you can see! (*To Guinevere*) Tell me, old thing. Does Richard Branson know you've borrowed one of his balloons? Haw! Haw! Haw!

Guinevere takes him by the ear and deposits him back on his throne

Guinevere Merlin! Announce the last entertainment of the evenin'!

She sits on her throne. Merlin stifling a yawn, bangs his wand

Merlin   Before you depart and become one day older,
                          May I present — Squirt, Sally and little Smoulder!

All clap and cheer as Squirt, Sally and Smoulder bounce on to do their act

The following are only suggestions. The actual comedy routine or speciality act is left to the individual director and talents of the three performers. (a) A comic ballet. (b) A mind reading act involving the cast and audience. (c) A balancing or juggling act. (d) A magic act, in which Merlin can intervene with some "real" magic. (e) If the theatre or hall has a raffle, it may be an idea to hold it here instead of during the interval or at the end of the show

After the routine, everyone cheers and applauds

Squirt, Sally and Smoulder take a bow, then exit

Merlin bangs his wand for silence

Merlin   That concludes the banquet at the midnight bell.
                          Your noble king will now bid you all farewell!

All turn towards Arthur. He is gazing into his goblet

Guinevere (*nudging him*) Arthur!

There is trouble brewing at Camelot! King Arthur has managed to escape Queen Guinevere's shopping trip but she will soon catch up with him. Meanwhile, Sally the kitchen maid is desperate to see her love, Squirty the squire but discovers he has a new female in his life — Smoulder the baby dragon. When the evil sorceress Morgana arrives with her son, Mordred, King Arthur will not listen to Merlin the wizard's sound advice and Arthur finds himself in a battle for his throne. Lancelot fights bravely but when Merlin's wand is transformed into a toilet brush, who will save him from the fire-breathing dragon? Paul Reakes' Camelot is a hilarious world of magical adventure — an Arthurian tale with a twist.

ISBN 0-573-06498-9

9 780573 064982

Arthur (*looking at her with a silly smile*) What is it, my little mint imperial?
Guinevere (*indicating the gathering*) Say somethin'! Say somethin'!
Arthur Righto! (*He gets to his feet and holds up his goblet*) Something!
Haw! Haw! Haw!

He flops back on to his throne

Guinevere (*to him, seething*) Oh, you're 'opeless! I suppose I'll 'ave to see
to it meself as usual! (*Regaining her composure and addressing the crowd*)
My 'usband and I — 'ope that you 'ave enjoyed this little "do", and thank
you all for comin'. It only remains for me to say — (*She rises and yells*)
Time gentlemen, please! Ain't you got no 'omes to go to?

The Chorus react and beat a hasty exit. Merlin and the Page exit R

Guinevere (*to Arthur*) Right, you! It's bed time!
Arthur What already, old thing? But the night is still young!
Guinevere Yes, but you're not! Come on! You know I need to get my eight
'ours beauty sleep!
Arthur (*aside to audience*) And *how* she needs it! (*He rises and goes to her*)
You go on up, old thing. I want to have a chat with Lancelot about his
adventures on the quest.
Guinevere You can do that in the mornin'! *Bed!*
Arthur (*standing up to her*) Now, you jolly well look here! I'm the queen…
er… the king! And if I want to stay up, I'm jolly well going to stay up! So
there!

Then he flinches away, fearing the worst!

Guinevere (*after taking a deep breath*) You can stay up for *five* minutes!
Arthur (*grovelling*) Yes, dear. Thank you, dear.
Guinevere But five minutes only!

She sweeps out R *followed by Olivia*

Arthur (*to the audience*) Haw! Haw! I showed her who was boss, didn't I?
Guinevere (*off* R, *bellowing*) Five minutes!

Arthur jumps with fright, then turns to Lancelot

Arthur Come on, old chap. Tell me all about your amazin' exploits on the
quest. (*He sits on his throne*) I want to hear every detail. I'm all ears!

Almost immediately, he falls fast asleep

Lancelot (*bowing*) Very well, sire.

He moves to L, *and faces front*

At this point, the lighting gradually dims, and becomes eerie and sinister. Weird sounds are heard faintly at first, then increasing in volume

Lancelot As you will recall, I set forth from Camelot on a Tuesday morning in July. It was a glorious day! The sun was shining, the birds were singing and I looked truly magnificent sitting on my horse in my brand new suit of armour. At midday, we halted at Ye Little Chefie (*or local place*) and partook of lunch. After lunch, we... we

He falters, obviously being affected by the changing atmosphere. He shakes his head to clear it, then continues

We continued on our journey. At four in the afternoon we... we (*He falters, becoming drowsy*) At four... in the... after... noon... we...

He lets his head fall forward for a few seconds, then raises it slowly. His face is now an expressionless mask, his eyes are fixed in a blank stare. He has fallen into a deep hypnotic trance. An eerie spotlight illuminates him

From out of the air, (an offstage microphone!) the evil laughter of Morgana is heard. Then her low, bewitching voice fills the stage and auditorium with its chilling malevolence

Morgana (*off, from the microphone*) Lancelot? Lancelot? Do you hear me?
Lancelot (*hypnotic voice*) I hear you.
Morgana (*off*) I am your master. You will obey my voice.
Lancelot I will obey your voice.
Morgana (*off*) Obey it now, Lancelot! Take your dagger and kill King Arthur while he sleeps! Do as I command! Obey me!
Lancelot I will obey!

Like a zombie, Lancelot takes out his dagger and holds it aloft. Morgana's laughter is heard

"Threatening" music creeps in

Lancelot, with dagger raised, turns and advances on the sleeping Arthur. He is about to strike

Merlin (*off* R, *calling loudly*) Sire! Sire!

The spell is instantly broken. The music and sounds stop abruptly. The lighting returns to normal. Lancelot snaps out of his trance. Arhur wakes up

   Merlin rushes on from R

     (*Alarmed*) Sire!
Arthur Merlin, old fruit! What's up? Is the jolly old castle on fire?
Merlin   Sire, forgive me bursting into the room,
                      But I have this feeling of impending doom!
Arthur Oh, it's probably something you ate at the banquet, old bean.
Merlin   My cause for concern is not indigestion!
                      Your majesty's safety is the matter in question!
                      I have this feeling which by degrees grows stranger,
                      It warns me you are in some imminent danger!
Arthur Danger? Haw! Haw! Haw! Not a bit of it! (*Rising*) Why I've got the
   bravest knight in all Camelot with me. (*He puts his hand on Lancelot's
   shoulder*) Good old Lancelot! No danger when he's about. He was just
   tellin' me about his adventures on the quest. Jolly thrillin' stuff too! Look,
   he's even got his dagger out! Re-enacting one of his battles! (*To Lancelot*)
   Weren't you, old boy?
Lancelot (*puzzled to find himself holding the dagger*) Er... yes, sire. (*He
   returns it to the scabbard*)

Arhur leads the perplexed Merlin to the R *exit*

Arthur Now, you toddle along like a good old wizard. Nothing for you to
   worry about.
Merlin But...
Arthur Take a couples of Rennies. You'll be as right as rain in the morning.
   Toodle pip!

He pushes Merlin off R, *then returns to his throne*

   Go on with your story, Lancelot. I'm listening. I'm all agog!

As before, he soon falls fast asleep

Lancelot (*bowing*) Certainly, sire. (*He moves to* L, *and faces front*)

At this point the lighting becomes sinister, and the sounds are heard as before

Now, where did I get to? Ah yes! At four in the afternoon it was time for tea. So we rode back to Ye Little Chefie (*or local place*) and partook of scones and toasted tea cakes. After tea we… we (*he falters, then continues as before*) we continued on our journey. At seven in the evening, we… we… (*he becomes drowsy as before*) At seven… in the…. evening, we…

Lancelot falls into a trance again, and is lit by a spotlight as before

Morgana's voice is heard. This time she is annoyed, to say the least!

Morgana (*off*) Lancelot? Lancelot? Do you hear me?
Lancelot I hear you.
Morgana (*off*) You failed to obey my command, Lancelot! Do not fail me a second time! Take your dagger and *kill* Arthur! Do it *now*!
Lancelot I will obey.

As before, Lancelot takes out his dagger, and advances on Arthur

"Threatening" music

He is about to strike

Olivia (*off* R, *calling*) Sire! Sire!

Again the spell is instantly broken

The lighting returns to normal. The music and sounds stop

Lancelot snaps out of his trance. Again he is puzzled to find himself holding the dagger

Olivia enters from R

Arthur wakes up, he does not see her

Arthur Not Merlin again! What does that bearded old buffoon want now? (*He turns and sees Olivia*) Oh, I say! You're not a bearded old buffoon, are you? (*He rises and goes to her*) Far from it! What can I do for you, my dear?
Olivia (*curtsying*) Sire. I come from her majesty the queen. She is most insistent that you retire to bed at once. She says that you have already had your extra five minutes. And if you don't come to bed immediately, she will ——

Arthur Yes, yes! I can imagine the rest! Oh, she can be frightfully difficult at times. (*Confidentially*) Between you and me, she can be a right pain in the portcullis!

Guinevere (*off* R, *bellowing*) I 'eard that! Arthur! Bed! Now!

Arthur (*cringing, then calling back*) Yes dear! Coming, dear! (*To them*) Better go. His master's voice! Toodle pip! (*To the audience*) Toodle pip!

Arthur scuttles out R

Olivia turns to Lancelot. He is replacing his dagger and looking rather perplexed

Olivia (*moving to him*) Lancelot? Are you all right?

Lancelot (*turning to her with a smile*) Of course I am. Why do you ask?

Olivia You seem a little distracted. Is there anything wrong?

Lancelot It's just that I feel… (*He momentarily touches his forehead, then pulls himself together, and laughs it off*) 'Tis nothing! It will soon pass.

Olivia (*smiling*) Too much wine at the banquet perhaps?

Lancelot (*mock shock*) You saucy wench! Are you suggesting I'm drunk? (*He gazes adoringly into her eyes*) Well, perhaps I am. (*He takes her in his arms*) But I'm not drunk on wine — I'm drunk on love! (*He sings*)

Song 11

A romantic duet with romantic lighting. They embrace at the end of the song

The Lights fade to Black-out

SCENE 2

Outside the Castle Walls

Tabs, on the frontcloth used in Act I, Scene 2

Sinister music and eerie lighting

Morgana and Mordred enter from DL

They are met with the usual storm of abuse

Mordred Well, that wasn't very successful, was it, Mummy?

Morgana (*snapping at him*) Oh, shut up, Mordred! Can I help it if those two fools came in and broke the spell! Arthur would be dead by now if they hadn't interfered!

Mordred You'd have been better off bewitching the (*local operatic or choral society*), and getting them to *sing* Arthur to death!
Morgana You stupid boy! (*Flaring at him*) Don't tell me how to do my job!
Mordred (*shrinking back*) No Mummy. Sorry Mummy. (*Slight pause*) I suppose we'd better go back to the castle and start packing.
Morgana Why?
Mordred Well, the magic potion didn't work, did it? And bewitching Lancelot hasn't worked either, so — not to put too fine a point on it, Mummy — you've lost!
Morgana (*snarling*) *Lost*! Oh, no, I haven't!

"Oh, yes you have!, Oh no I haven't!" routine with her and the audience

Mordred (*to her, timidly*) I — I think they could be right, Mummy.
Morgana (*beside herself with rage*) *Right*! *Right*! How can *they* be right? They're just a miserable mob of mindless morons! And *you*, Mordred! You're such a defeatist! Just like your wretched father! But I sorted him out! I turned him into a (*local football or cricket team*) supporter! And now he feels *permanently* defeated! Ha! Ha! Ha! (*Turning on Mordred*) Take care you don't suffer the same fate, my son!
Mordred (*shrinking back*) S-Sorry Mummy. (*Slight pause*) What are you going to try next?
Morgana I intend to have one more attempt at getting Lancelot to kill Arthur for us. If *that* fails, I have another diabolical plan up my sleeve!
Mordred (*excitedly trying to look up her sleeve*) Where is it? Where is it?

She slaps his hand away

Morgana You stupid boy!
Mordred (*rubbing his sore hand*) I only want to know what your other plan is! What is it, Mummy?
Morgana I shall not divulge it in front of this — (*to the audience*) *rabble of rubbish*!

By-play with audience

(*Then to Mordred*) Let us be gone from here! I have to summon all my powers and put Lancelot into another trance! Come, Mordred!

Amid boos and hisses, they exit DR

The lighting changes to give a cold, moonlight effect

Smoulder scampers on from DL *to* C *she gives the audience a wave*

Squirt (*off* L, *calling*) Smoulder! Where are you? Smoulder!

Smoulder scampers off DR

Squirt enters from DL. *He is comically dressed in a night-cap and very short night-shirt*

(*Calling*) Smoulder! Oh, where's she gone now? (*Shivering*) Brr! It's flippin' freezin' out 'ere! And me in me short shift too! (*To someone in the front row*) Oy! What are *you* lookin' at? (*Business with pulling the front of his shirt down*) Stop tryin' to peek under my pinny! You rude thing, you!

By-play with the audience

Sally (*off* L, *calling*) Squirty! Where are you?
Squirt (*calling back*) Over here, Sally! (*To the audience*) If you think *I* look funny — Get a load of this!

Sally enters from DL, *she is wearing an outrageous pink pyjama suit*

(*To the audience*) "Barbie" comes to (*local place!*) (*or some other topical gag to suit*)
Sally Have you found Smoulder yet, Squirty?
Squirt Does it look like it? She's a naughty little scamp! (*To the audience*) D'you know, we were just gettin' into bed...
Sally (*acting coy*) Oh, Squirtykins!
Squirt Separately, I might add! And Smoulder decides she wants to go outside and... er... you know!
Sally (*to the audience*) Dig an 'ole! So she could...
Squirt (*to Sally*) All right! All right! You don't 'ave to explain 'er every little movement! (*To the audience*) We let 'er out, and waited on the doorstep, but she didn't come back!
Sally So, we went outside to look for her, an' when we turned around, they'd locked the castle doors!
Squirt And we were shut out in the freezin' cold! In just our jimjams! (*He shivers*) Brr! Now I know just how a penguin feels!

Business with pulling his shirt down

Sally Coo! Squirty! 'Aven't you got sexy legs!

Squirt Legs? They feel more like icicles! If I stand out 'ere much longer, people will think I've escaped from one of Tesco's freezers!

Sally I'm cold too. (*Sidling up to him*) Squirty, why don't we snuggle together and keep each other warm?

Squirt Well, I suppose anythin's better than gettin' frozen assets!

Sally grabs him and hugs him tightly against her

Sally Is that better?

Squirt (*a breathless squeak*) Yes!

Sally Mmm! This is nice! Mmm! I feel warm all over! (*Pause*) Squirty?

Squirt Yes, Sally?

Sally What about that little thing between us?

Squirt Eh?

Sally Is it still on?

Squirt (*pulling away from her*) I 'ope so! It's not *that* cold!

Sally What's the cold got to do with it? I'm talkin' about our engagement!

Squirt Oh! (*Relieved*) Phew!

Sally You said we'd get engaged as soon as you got back from the quest.

Squirt Do I... I mean, did I?

Sally Yes, you did! You said you'd give me a ring!

Squirt And I will! Just as soon as someone invents the telephone! It's good to talk!

Sally Squirty, you do still *want* to marry me, don't you?

Squirt Of course I do, Sally. It's just that... well...

Sally Well, what?

Squirt I'm still only a poor, underpaid squire. It might be years before I become a Knight of the Round Table! What are we gonna live on in the meantime?

Sally (*passionately*) The *fruits* of love!

She throws her arms around him, and squeezes him tightly

Squirt (*wincing*) Ooogh! I 'ate to tell you, but you've just squashed a couple of the plums!

Sally Oh, Squirty! I can just picture us when we're married! We'll be just like (*current romantic couple on TV, or in the news*)!

Squirt (*to the audience*) More like (*current unromantic couple*)!

Song 12

A comedy duet

At the end of the song Squirt makes his escape DR, *with Sally pursuing him. Smoulder scampers on from* DL, *waves to the audience, and follows them off* DR

The Lights fade to Black-out

SCENE 3

The Royal Bedchamber

An insert half-set. The back and side walls are printed to represent the Castle interior with arched window R. *Comic portraits of Arthur and Guinevere hang over the bed, there is a dented suit of armour, and a cupboard with clothes spilling out, etc. There is a practical archway in the* L *wall. A double bed is set* C, *with its foot facing the audience*

Guinevere is discovered sitting on the end of the bed. She wears a voluminous, frilly dressing-gown and her hair is in plaits. She is gazing adoringly into a large hand mirror, and singing "Lovely to look at, etc." to herself. Suddenly she becomes aware of the audience and jumps up with a shriek

Guinevere Aaagh! What are you lot doin' in the Royal Boudoir? (*She comes forward to the mirror*) Where do you think you are, (*Royal reference*)? Oh! And there's *men* 'ere too! (*Coyly rearranging her gown*) Oh, you naughty boys! You shouldn't be seein' me in this state! (*Archly*) And the first one to say I shouldn't be seen in *any* state, gets a thick ear! (*She looks in the mirror, and strokes her cheek*) I've just finished my night-time preparation, girls. Well you've got to keep those wrinkles at bay, (*to someone, pointedly*) 'aven't you, dear? Oh, I slap the lot on, y'know! Nivea's Village! The one with those Hippodromes! Pollyfilla! And what's that other one called? Oh, yes — Oil of Ugly! I use the lot! But it's worth it. (*She looks adoringly into the mirror*) Ah, yes! The face that munched a thousand chips! Look! (*She holds the mirror out to the audience*) I've got the face of a sixteen year old! (*Archly*) Who said I bet she was glad to get rid of it? I tried a face lift once, but it didn't work! Every time I blinked, I pulled me stockin's down! But I don't know why I bother, really I don't. My Arthur doesn't seem to notice me anymore! There was a time when 'e used to chase me around the Round Table every night! Now 'e just 'ides under it! But tonight is gonna be different, girls! Oh, yes! I'm feeling all Mills an' Boony! (*She hangs the mirror on the wall* R, *and preens herself and calls very sweetly*) Yoo hoo! Arthur, dear! Are you comin' to bedy-byes?
Arthur (*off* L) Coming, old thing!

Guinevere adopts what she thinks is a very sexy, seductive pose!

Arthur enters from L. *He wears a long red night-shirt, decorated with gold "AR" motifs. He still wears his crown*

(*Spotting the audience, and waving to them*) What ho!

The audience call back

Arthur notices Guinevere's pose

By Jove! Guinie, old thing! Are you all right?

Guinevere (*seductively*) Just waiting for you — lover boy!

Arthur Oh, good show! I thought you'd been struck by lightning or something! Haw! Haw! Haw!

Guinevere is deflated, and drops the pose

The Page enters from L *carrying Excalibur. He gives a loud sniff*

Guinevere (*to the audience*) That's all we need! The human vacuum cleaner!

Nonchalantly, the Page goes to the bed, and pulls back the covers. He puts Excalibur in the middle of the bed and replaces the covers. Guinevere watches this ceremony with great disdain

The Page bows to Arthur, gives an extra loud sniff, and exits L

Oh, Arthur! Must we always 'ave that overgrown toothpick in bed *with* us?

Arthur Of course, old thing! Trusty Excalibur must be by my side at all times, don't y'know!

Guinevere But it's so dangerous! I could roll over in the night and sever my connections! To say nothin' of slashin' me prices an' cuttin' me losses! Besides — (*she sits on* R *end of the bed*) It's not very *romantic*, is it?

Arthur (*sitting on* L *end of the bed*) Romantic? What d'you mean, old fruit?

Guinevere (*to the audience*) See! 'E's even forgot what the word means!(*She slides nearer to him*) In the old days you always put your sword *under* the bed.

Arthur Yes, but it got so frightfully dusty. A weapon's not much use if it's covered in cobwebs, is it?

Guinevere (*to the audience*) There's no answer to that!

Sliding up close to him

Arthur, do you remember the pet names you used to call me by?

She puts her head on his shoulder

Your little bunny rabbit! Your little lamb! Do you remember?
Arthur Yes! (*To the audience*) And over the years the animals have got bigger and bigger! Haw! Haw! Haw!
Guinevere (*throwing her arms around him*) Oh, Arthur, dearest! Tonight is so full of romance! There's somethin' in the air! Can't you sense it?
Arthur (*after a couple of sniffs*) Yes, I jolly well can! I think that dashed moat needs cleanin' out again!
Guinevere (*hugging him tightly*) Oh, Arthur! My beloved! Take me in your arms an' whisper sweet nothin's in me shell like!

She buries his face into her chest and holds it there while he squirms to get free

Oh! This night was made for love! *I* want to be loved! Can't you feel my 'eart poundin'! *Poundin'*! Oh, Arthur!

Arthur manages to resurface and gasps for air

Oh, I'm *suffocated* with love! My breath'll only come in short pants!
Arthur (*gasping*) You're lucky! Mine'll only come in (*gasp*) long trousers!
Guinevere (*releasing him and proclaiming dramatically*) Oh! I'm burning with the fires of passion! And you're the man with the hose pipe! (*She throws out her arms, preparing to hug him again*) Oh, my Romeo!
Arthur Oh, not again!

He leaps from the bed. Guinevere, hugging thin air, crashes to the floor. Arthur tries to exit L, but she grabs his ankle. She hauls herself up on his nightshirt

Guinevere Arthur, you may be a ruler of men, but 'ere's a *woman* who needs dominatin'! (*She hugs him in a bear like grip*) But please, be gentle with me!
Arthur B —But I've got a headache, old thing!
Guinevere (*spinning him around*) A headache? You'll soon forget about that!

She pushes him back on to the bed. To the conductor or pianist

Hit it!

Song 13

"The Stripper" strikes up, and the Lights dim. Lit by a follow spot, Guinevere goes into her comic striptease. As soon as it starts, Arthur crawls into bed (left side) and pulls the covers over his head. Under her dressing-gown are layers of comic corsets, bras and knickers, etc. As she discards each item she throws it off stage DL *or* DR. *To end, she wears outrageous underwear with a comic slogan across her chest or seat*

She strikes a pose on the last note of music, and the lighting returns to normal

Guinevere (*to the audience*) There! That's bound to 'ave got 'is pulses racin'! (*To someone in the front row*) And yours *too*, by the look of it! (*She slinks up to the bed*) I bet that's taken your mind off yer 'eadache, eh, Arthur?

A loud snore comes from Arthur. Guinevere reacts and gets annoyed

(*To the audience*) Well! Would you Adam an' Eve it? I might as well 'ave read the last chapter of me Catherine Cookson!

Grumbling she stomps around to her side of the bed and climbs in. She gives a yell of pain

Aaaagh! (*She looks under the covers*) Oh, that flippin' sword! It's like sleeping with Edward Scissor'ands (*She lies down, then sits up again*) There's a terrible draught comin' through that blinkin' window again!

She digs and pokes Arthur

Arthur! Arthur, wake up!
Arthur (*sitting up with a start, still half asleep*) Oh, stop it, Madonna! (*or current female personality*). You know I'm ticklish… Oh! What's ——
Guinevere There's a draught comin' through that window again! I shan't sleep a wink all night! Change sides!

Comic business as they get out of bed and change sides. They lie down and very soon are snoring in unison

The lighting grows dark and eerie. Morgana's voice is heard (an offstage microphone)

Morgana (*off*) Lancelot? Lancelot?

Lancelot appears in the archway L, *lit by an eerie follow spot. He is in a trance again and walks forward like a zombie*

Do you hear me?
Lancelot I hear you.
Morgana You will not disobey my voice a third time, Lancelot! Do you understand?
Lancelot I understand.
Morgana Go and strangle Arthur while he sleeps! Do it *now!*
Lancelot I will obey.

Holding out his hands before him, he advances towards the left side of the bed

"Threatening" music creeps in

He reaches down and proceeds to throttle Guinevere. She wakes up and starts yelling and thrashing about

Guinevere *Aaagh...! Help...! Ooow...! Aaagh!*

Arthur wakes, sits up and sees what is happening

Arthur Lancelot!

The spell is instantly broken

The lighting returns to normal. The music stops, and Lancelot snaps out of his trance

He is dumbfounded to see his hands around Guinevere's throat and hastily takes them away. She coughs and splutters

Merlin and Olivia rush on from L

Merlin   We heard such yells and screams most dire!
                    Tell us! What has happened, sire?
Arthur (*getting out of bed, bewildered*) Well, I don't rightly know, old bean. I woke up and found young Lancelot tryin' to throttle the missus!
Olivia (*rushing to Lancelot*) Lancelot! Is this true?
Lancelot (*totally confused*) I don't know! One minute I was in my own room, the next I was here... with my hands around her majesty's throat...
Arthur Gave her a pretty nasty fright too! Not used to bein' manhandled in your own bed, are you, old thing?

Guinevere (*giving him a look*) You can say that again!
Lancelot (*to Guinevere*) I beg your majesty's pardon. I honestly have no idea
what came over me. Please forgive me for laying my hands upon you.
Guinevere Oh, anytime! I mean ——
Arthur I know what happened! You were sleepwalking Lancelot! That's it!
Sleepwalking and dreaming you were killing another old dragon! (*He
points to Guinevere and laughs*) Haw! Haw! Haw!
Guinevere (*indignantly*) Thank *you*!
Arthur I'm sure that's the explanation. Now we can all toddle off back to
our beds, what.
Merlin   Sire, I fear 'tis not so cut and dried!
                            Some *evil influence* has here been tried!
Arthur (*to the others*) Oh, crikey! Old doom and gloom's off again!
Merlin   Remember I gave you a warning tip...
Arthur   Yes, you did! Now let's get some kip!

He is about to climb back into bed

Merlin   Wait!
                   My premonition has been proved right!
                   Evil powers are at work this night!
                   'Tis my belief that Lancelot is spellbound!
                   He's been bewitched by a devious hell hound!
                   The task of *murder* was sent to inflict him,
                   But the *queen* was not the intended victim!
                   Put in a trance and against his will,
                   'Twas the *king* he was supposed to kill!

Reaction from the others. Guinevere leaps out of bed and rushes to Arthur

Lancelot (*horrified*) Bewitched! But that means I could still be a danger to
his majesty's life! You'd better lock me up at once!
Merlin   For that precaution there will be no need.
                            I shall remove the spell with all due speed

He raises his wand

                   O Spell of Evil that bewitches this knight
                   I command you be gone! This instant! *Take flight!*

He points his wand at Lancelot

There is a flash and a puff of smoke

Lancelot staggers and holds his head. Olivia supports him. Soon he recovers, and smiles to indicate he is himself once more

Olivia (*to the others*) Who could be vile enough to cast such an evil spell on
  Lancelot?
Arthur Yes! Who *is* the rotter?
Merlin   Sire, who would like to see you dead?
                    Who would seize the crown from your head?
                    Who has the charm of a hungry piranha?
                    That cousin of yours! The evil Morgana!

There is a flash of lightning and a great roll of thunder. The lighting becomes dark and sinister

Arthur and Guinevere cling to each other, as do Lancelot and Olivia. Morgana's evil laughter fills the stage and auditorium. (An offstage microphone) Note: at this point Guinevere and Olivia need to be fairly close to an exit

Morgana Ha! Ha! Ha! The old fool is right! It was *I*, Morgana the Mighty,
  who bewitched Lancelot! He was supposed to kill you, Arthur! But he
  failed! Now I will have to put my other plan into action! Ha! Ha! Ha! (*She
  casts her evil spell*)
                    O Powers of darkness and sorcery,
                    Come to my aid and work for me!
                    Remove the two females without any hassle,
                    And transfer them both to my secret castle! Ha! Ha! Ha!

Her laughter continues. There is a flash of lightning and a roll of thunder. Black-out

  Under cover of darkness, Guinevere and Olivia exit

When the Lights come back up, they appear to have vanished. Arthur and Lancelot have their arms around thin air

Arthur (*gaping at the empty space*) Guinie? Where are you, old thing?
Lancelot Olivia? Where are they? What's happened to them?
Morgana Ha! Ha! Ha! I have transported them to my castle beyond the
  enchanted forest! They are now my prisoners! Tonight they will suffer
  hideous tortures, and then — *die*! Ha! Ha! Ha!
Arthur (*getting his dander up*) Oh, I say! This isn't cricket, y'know! Merlin,
  don't just stand there! *Do* something! Bring 'em back at once!

Morgana It is too late! The old fool is powerless! He can do nothing to reverse my spell!

Merlin   Alas, the things she says are true.
                          I'm just as helpless as the pair of you!

Lancelot Sire! There is only one thing to be done! We must go to Morgana's castle at once and rescue the queen and Olivia.

Morgana Ha! Ha! Ha! (*Mockingly*) Brave words, Sir Knight. You are quite welcome to try! Come by all means — if you dare! Ha! Ha! Ha!

Her laughter fades away, and the lighting returns to normal

Arthur (*in a dither*) Er… where's my armour? Merlin! Summon the Tights of the Round Navel! Er… Call for the…

Lancelot I'm afraid there isn't time for all that, sire! (*He goes to exit* L) We must go at once if we've any hope of saving them!

Arthur Right ho!

Merlin   Sire, is it wise to go in such a flap?
                          You could be walking straight into a trap!

Arthur What other choice is there, old fruit? Lead on, Lancelot! To the jolly old rescue!

Lancelot dashes out L, *Arthur follows, then pauses to wave to the audience*

Toodle pip!

He runs out L. *Merlin shakes his head woefully, then trots out after him*

The Lights fade to Black-out

SCENE 4

On the Edge of the Enchanted Forest

Tabs, or a front cloth showing twisted trees and dense undergrowth

Moonlight effect

Smoulder scampers on from DR *to* C

Squirt ⎫
Sally ⎬ (*together; off, calling*) Smoulder! Smoulder! Where are you?
           ⎭

Smoulder scampers to DL *exit, but Squirt enters there*

Squirt Ah! Got ya!

Smoulder scampers to DR exit, but Sally enters there

Sally Ah! Got ya!

They close in on Smoulder and bring her to C

Squirt Thank goodness for that! We've been 'untin' 'igh an' low for you!
Sally Yes! We've been locked out of Camelot because of you! You're a very naughty little dragon! That's what *you* are! (*To the audience*) Isn't she naughty, boys and girls?

Smoulder shakes her head at the audience, encouraging them to disagree. "Oh, yes she is! Oh, no she isn't!" routine with the audience

Squirt Well, now that we've found Smoulder we ought to get back to Camelot and hope they'll open for us.
Sally (*looking around, scared*) Y-Yes! I don't like this place. It's c- creepy! We're right on the edge of the Enchanted Forest! And there's only one place spookier than that!
Squirt Yes! The (*local reference*)!
Sally No! Morgana's Castle! It's just on the other side of those trees! She might creep out of the bushes and take us unaware!
Squirt Take our underwear!
Sally And then *grab us* by the undergrowth!
Squirt (*pulling down the front of his shirt*) Eeeek! You're right Sally! Let's get away from 'ere! Let's go back to Camelot!
Sally Lead on then.
Squirt No, after you. Age before beauty.
Sally But I insist!
Squirt No, ladies first!

An awkward pause

Sally Squirty?
Squirt Yes, Sally?
Sally You don't know the way *back* to Camelot, do you? You're lost!
Squirt (*blustering*) Lost? *Me*? Never! I know every inch of this place! They don't call me the Indiana Jones of (*local place*) for nothin'! I know this place like the back of my 'and!

He turns away and peers at the back of his hand

(*To the audience*) What a pity I 'ad a wash this mornin'!

Sally Well, which way *is* it?

Squirt (*floundering*) It's… er… er (*he crosses his arms and points to left and right*) *that* way!

Sally (*on the verge of tears*) I knew it! I knew it! We're lost! Lost in the wicked wood!

Squirt Now keep calm, Sally! Don't get hysterical! Perhaps Smoulder knows the way. (*To Smoulder*) Do you know the way back to Camelot?

Smoulder shrugs, and shakes her head

Sally (*wailing*) Waaagh! *We're lost*!

Squirt Don't be a silly Sally! It's *got* to be *this* way!

He takes her by the hand and leads her to DL *then stops*

No! I think it's *that* way!

He drags her across to DR *then stops*

No! I'm sure it's *this* way!

He drags her to DL *then stops. He repeats this business a few more times, dragging the sobbing Sally with him*

During the business, Smoulder sneaks away and exits DL

(*Finally giving up and moving to* C) Oh, it's no use! I give up! I don't know which way it is! You're right, Sally, we're lost! (*He puts his arm around her*) But fear not! Me and my frozen kneecaps are here to protect you!

Sally Oh, Squirtykins! Can't we just get away from 'ere? Anywhere would be better than 'angin' about near this nasty forest!

Squirt Right! We'll go *that* way! (*He points* R) Come on, Smoulder. (*He looks around*) Smoulder? Oh, no! She's done a bunk again! (*To the audience*) Which way did she go, kids? Did she go *that way*? (*He points to* DL)

"Yes!" from audience

Oh, crumbs! That means she's gone into the forest! (*To Sally*) We'll 'ave to go and get 'er, or the queen'll 'ave our guts for garters!

Sally Well, *I'm* not goin' into that 'orrid, spooky forest! I bet it's full of monsters and *slimy creepy crawlies*!

Squirt As I 'ope to become a knight of the Round Table one day, I've got to get used to facin' dangers!

He steels himself and struts to DL, *then stops, nervously*

Slimy creepy crawlies, did you say?
Sally Yes! And *grisly ghosts and vicious vampires!*

Squirt gulps. He steels himself again, struts to DL *then chickens out at the last minute and runs back to Sally*

Squirt What shall we do, Sally?
Sally I don't know, Squirty!

Low, evil laughter (Mordred) is heard from off DR

Squirt and Sally react and cling to each other in terror

W-W-What w-was that?
Squirt I d-d-didn't hear anything!

The laughter is repeated, louder

The two quake with fear

(*Gulping*) I didn't hear *that* either! Oooo! (*His knees start to knock. To the audience*) I… Is there something nasty behind us, kids?

"No!" from the audience

Sally (*to the audience*) Y-You'll tell us if you *do* see something, won't you?

Mordred sneaks on from DR, *and creeps up behind them*

The audience will be shouting "He's behind you, etc.!" Business with Squirt and Sally turning with Mordred keeping behind them. Eventually they discover him standing between them. They yell and try to make a run for it, but he grabs them

Mordred So! What have we got here? Wallace and Gromit, is it? Well, hard cheese! Ha! Ha! Ha! (*He calls off* R) Mummy! Come and see what *I've* found!

Morgana sweeps on from DR, *and gives her evil laugh*

Morgana Ha! Ha! Ha!
Squirt Oh, no! It's Cruella de Ville! (*Or current unpopular female*)
Morgana Excellent! Lancelot's squire and the kitchen maid! Well done,
  Mordred! Take them to our castle and lock them up with Guinevere and her
  lady-in-waiting!
Sally Did you hear that, Squirty? She's viaducted the queen and Lady Olivia!
Squirt (*to Morgana*) You won't get away with this, you — you *person*, you!
  King Arthur is bound to come to their rescue!
Morgana Exactly! That's what I'm counting on! Ha! Ha! Ha! Take them
  away, Mordred!
Mordred Yes, Mummy!

He drags the protesting Squirt and wailing Sally out DL

Morgana Ha! Ha! Ha! (*To the audience*) Those two nitwits will serve as
  extra bait for Arthur. Oh, my plan is so clever in its simplicity. By
  kidnapping the queen I will lure Arthur away from the safety of Camelot.
  Alone, without the protection of his knights, he will be easy prey! Ha! Ha!
  And when I've finished with him, I will come down and sort *you* out!

By-play with audience, then she looks off R

  Ah! Excellent! I see Arthur and Lancelot approaching! (*She moves to* C)
        Let them both hurry to my castle gate!
        Alone and unarmed they will soon meet their fate!
        To those two "heroes" you can bid a last farewell!
        I am going to feed them to my creatures from Hell!

*Spreading her arms and throwing back her head, she laughs with demonic
glee*

  Ha! Ha! Ha!

*There is a blinding flash of lightning and a great roll of thunder. Howling
wind and weird sounds fill the air*

  Laughing her terrible laugh, Morgana sweeps out DL

The Lights fade to Black-out

The thunder and weird sounds, etc., continue into the next scene

SCENE 5

The Gateway to Morgana's Castle

A dark and sinister place, full of evil atmosphere. Raised, back C, and silhouetted against a blood red cyclorama, is the gateway. Supposedly fashioned from rock, it resembles the grotesque head of a giant demon with horns, slanted eyes and a gaping mouth that forms the entrance. There are twisted trees and jagged rocks at the sides

To suitable creepy music, the eerie lighting comes up to reveal the sinister scene. Ground mist swirls, thunder rolls, and a flash of lightning illuminates the fearful gateway

From out of the darkness and mist, the Chorus and Dancers shuffle on as Morgana's army of ghastly Ghouls. They perform a strange, jerky song and dance

Song 14

After the song, there is a flash of lightning and a roll of thunder

Morgana appears in the gateway lit by a green follow spot, laughing her evil laugh

The Ghouls turn US. With grunts and jerky bows, they pay homage to her. She descends, and they gather around her

Morgana Ah, my flesh eating fiends! I trust you are feeling as ravenous as ever?
1st Ghoul (*grunting and pointing to its mouth*) Hun-gry! Hun-gry!
2nd Ghoul (*doing the same*) Foood! Flesh! Hu-man flesh!
All Ghouls (*in a grunted chant*) Flesh! Flesh! We want flesh! Flesh! Flesh! We want ——
Morgana (*raising her arms*) Enough!

The Ghouls cower back and go silent

Be patient, my cannibalistic cronies! Very soon there will be plenty of human flesh for you to sink your teeth into!

The Ghouls grunt their appreciation

But first, you must conceal yourselves and await my signal! *Go*!

The Ghouls shuffle to the sides, and exit R *and* L

Morgana comes forward

Ha! Ha! Ha! (*To the audience, mockingly*) Poor Arthur and Lancelot. Little
do they realize that they are "Today's Special" on my Ghouls menu! (*She
looks off* DR) Ah! Here they come! All ready to be served up! Ha! Ha! Ha!

She sweeps US, *and exits through the gateway. There is a flash of lightning,
and the wind and weird sounds fade out*

Lancelot and Arthur enter, very cautiously from DR

Arthur   (*to the audience, in a whisper*) What ho!

The audience answer

Lancelot   (*pointing out the gateway*) Look! There it is, sire! The gateway to
Morgana's castle!
Arthur   By Jove! What an absolutely frightful shocker! (*To the audience*) I
thought (*reference to some new local building or development, etc.*) was
pretty rum, but *this* place takes the jolly old biscuit, what?
Lancelot   Come, sire!

Lancelot is about to advance US

Arthur   (*holding Lancelot back*) Hang on, Lancelot! Hadn't we better wait
for Merlin? Can't understand what's keepin' the old blighter! Thought he
was right behind us.
Lancelot   We can't afford to wait, sire. A moment's delay could mean certain
death for Queen Guinevere and Olivia.
Arthur   You know we're unarmed, don't you, old bean? I completely forgot
to bring Excalibur with me!
Lancelot   I realize that, sire. We'll just have to fight it out with our bare hands!
Arthur   Oh, really? (*Rolling up his sleeves*) Righto, then! Let's go for it!
Tally-ho!

Before they can advance, there is a flash of lightning and a crash of thunder

Morgana appears in the gateway, in green spotlight

Morgana Ha! Ha! Ha! So! The great Arthur and brave Sir Lancelot have
come visiting, eh?

Arthur (*as if to a child*) Now, come along, Morgana. Stop all this
naughtiness and be a good girl. Release Guinevere and Olivia at once.

Morgana And give you a wasted journey? Oh no. You came here to rescue
them. I don't want to spoil your fun! (*She moves to one side and calls
through the gateway*) Mordred!

Mordred appears in the gateway

Mordred Yes, Mummy?

Morgana Bring them out!

Mordred Yes, Mummy!

He disappears

*Guinevere, Olivia, Squirt and Sally are pushed through the gateway. They
huddle together in a terrified group. Mordred enters behind them*

Arthur Guinie!

Guinevere Arthur!

Lancelot Olivia!

Olivia Lancelot!

Sally (*to the audience*) Daddy!

Squirt Anybody! (*Or the name of someone known to be in the audience*)

Guinevere Arthur! Don't stand there like a stick of rhubarb! Come and save
me at once!

Morgana (*mockingly*) Yes, Arthur. Come and save your little damsel in
distress. Wasn't that what you came here to do?

Arthur Yes, and I'm jolly well going to! Come on, Lancelot!

He and Lancelot are about to move US

Olivia Wait! Please be careful! It might be a trap!

They stop, and Arthur brings Lancelot back to DR

Arthur (*to Lancelot*) I say, do you think she could be right?

Lancelot I'm not sure, sire! (*To the audience*) What do you think? Do *you*
think it's a trap?

"Yes!" from audience

Arthur (*to the audience*) Are you absolutely sure, old things?

"Yes!" from audience

(*To Lancelot*) They seem pretty sure, don't they?
Morgana (*to Guinevere and the others, mockingly*) Oh dear, oh dear! It
doesn't look as if you're going to be rescued after all. Your two *heroes* have
turned into *snivelling cowards*!
Arthur I say! She called us snivellin' cowards! I'm not standing for that!
Come on, old chap! Let's jolly well go and get 'em!
Lancelot I'm right behind you, sire!
Arthur Stout fellow! But not *too* far behind, what?

*They advance to about midstage. Morgana raises her arms and shouts a
command*

Morgana Now!

There is a flash of lightning and a roll of thunder. Ground mist appears

    The Ghouls enter from both sides to suitable music

*Arthur and Lancelot see them and halt in their tracks. Grunting their chant
of "Flesh! Flesh! etc.", the Ghouls completely surround Arthur and Lancelot.
Guinevere and the others are crying out in terror*

                Soon I will be rid of you meddlesome fools!
                I'm going to feed you to my flesh eating ghouls!
                To delay any longer would be a sin!
                So! Dinner is served — *get stuck in*!

*With clawing fingers and hungry slavering noises, the Ghouls advance on
Arthur and Lancelot*

    There is a flash, a puff of smoke and Merlin appears DR

Merlin (*as he appears*) Hold!

This stops the Ghouls dead in their tracks

                You undead creatures! You evil slaves!
                I command you return at once to your graves!
    Begone!

He points his wand at the Ghouls

There is a flash. Weird lights (strobe, perhaps?) flash across the stage

The Ghouls recoil and run out with panic-stricken howls

The lighting returns to previous setting

Morgana and Mordred beat a hasty exit through the gateway

Guinevere and the others rush down to join Arthur and Lancelot

Squirt Sire! Lancelot! Morgana and 'er son 'ave gone! They've done a runner!
Lancelot Good riddance! We're all safe now, that's the main thing.

He embraces Olivia

Guinevere (*embracing Arthur*) Oh, Arthur! Me whole life flashed before me! All twenty one years of it! Just fancy! A second later and you might 'ave been gobbled up by the ghoulies!
Arthur Well, I'm safe now, old tulip! We all are! Thanks to Merlin! Well done, my good old wizard.
Merlin (*bowing*) Thank you, sire. I aim to be of service.
                         Can we go now? This place still makes me nervous.
Arthur Right you are! (*To the others*) Come on, you chaps. Let's get back to jolly old Camelot.

Suddenly Morgana sweeps on from L, followed by Mordred

Morgana *Not so fast!* I haven't finished with you yet, Arthur! I still mean to destroy you and become ruler of Britain!
Arthur (*peeved*) Oh, I say! You're not *still* at it, are you? You're being an absolute bounder, y'know! Do something, Merlin. Send them to (*nearby town or village*), or somewhere!
Merlin   To send them *there* would suit us well!
                         Just let me cast the appropriate spell!

He moves near to the R wings, holds up the wand in his right hand and prepares to cast a spell. Quickly Morgana makes some magic passes at him

There is a flash. Weird lights (strobe?) flash across the stage. The others cry out in fear and confusion

When the lighting returns to normal, Merlin is seen holding up a toilet brush instead of his wand! (Note: The switch is effected from the wings during the flashing lights, etc. and hopefully unseen by the audience!) They all gape in astonishment at the brush, not least Merlin himself. Morgana and Mordred laugh with devilish glee

Morgana Ha! Ha! Ha! The wand has vanished! And so have Merlin's powers!
Arthur (*to Merlin*) Is that true?
Merlin (*nodding, sadly*)
　　　　　　Without the wand my powers are at an end!
　　　　　　I'm only good for —
　　　　　　(*Holding up the brush*) Cleaning around the bend!
Morgana (*with evil glee*) You are now at Mummy's mercy! And has *she* got a surprise for *you*!
Lancelot (*to Morgana*) What devilry do you intend this time?
Morgana Something you have encountered before, Sir Knight. But this time you will face it *without* the protection of your sword and armour! It's a——
Mordred (*pleading*) Please let *me* tell them, Mummy! Please! Please!
Morgana Oh, very well, my little soldier.
Mordred (*to the others, with evil relish*) It's a — *fire breathing dragon*!

He and his mother laugh their evil laughs. Shock horror from the others. Morgana steps forward and raises her arms

Morgana　　　　Come forth my serpent of fire and smoke!
　　　　　　　　　Your killing powers I now — *invoke*!

Monstrous roars and bellows are heard, filling the stage and auditorium. From off L, there is a blinding flash of light and a jet of smoke issues forth

Arthur and the others cower away to R. Morgana and Mordred are DL. The roars get louder

A huge fearsome-looking Dragon enters from UL

Terrified yells from the group. The Dragon moves to C and turns its head in Morgana's direction

　　(*Commanding it, and pointing to the group*) Destroy them! Destroy them all!

With a roar, the Dragon advances on the terrified group

Suitable dramatic music

Lancelot boldly steps in front of the beast and confronts it with raised fists. With one swipe of its claw, the Dragon knocks Lancelot aside. The knight is instantly on his feet again and, moving behind the creature, gives it a hefty kick on the rear. With a roar, the Dragon turns on Lancelot and advances on him to C. *They grapple. Lancelot is knocked to the ground. The Dragon roars and towers over the fallen knight*

   (*To the Dragon*) Burn him! Burn him to a crisp!

The Dragon takes an enormous breath as if preparing to breathe out fire

   Suddenly Smoulder scampers on from L

She stops and looks at the Dragon. It stops and looks at her. Smoulder makes little questioning noises. The Dragon does the same. They both nod, then Smoulder rushes to the Dragon. They cuddle fondly, and make affectionate little noises. Lancelot jumps to his feet and joins the others. All are in a state of bewilderment

Arthur Merlin, you understand Dragonese! What's goin' on?
Merlin   It appears these beasts are related to each other.
             She is Smoulder's long lost mother!

General reaction

Smoulder nods her head and hugs the Dragon. Her mother strokes Smoulder's head, then turns to Merlin and "talks" to him in a series of grunts, squawks and growls. Nodding, he appears to understand perfectly

            It seems she was captured from her dragon's lair,
            And made to work for that evil pair!
            She's not seen her child for over a year,
            And during that time has shed many a tear.
            But now reunited with her little waif,
            She thanks us all for keeping her safe.
            She's pleased to see her in such fine fettle,
            And with Morgana she now has a score to settle!

The Dragon gives a terrifying roar and advances slowly on Morgana and Mordred

Mordred (*terrified*) M-M-Mummy!
Morgana (*trying to command the Dragon*) Back! Back, I say!

The Dragon continues to advance on them

Mordred I don't think it's listening, Mummy!

The Dragon takes in an enormous breath

    Oh, no! It's going to breathe fire!
Morgana Run, Mordred, run!

They run off L. The Dragon follows them out

From off L there is a blinding flash, a loud explosion and a great cloud of smoke billows out. (Note: during this diversion, Merlin surreptitiously exchanges the toilet brush for his wand) The lighting becomes much brighter

The Dragon enters, dusts off her claws, and goes back to Smoulder

Squirt runs off L and returns holding up two pairs of "smoking" boots

Squirt Cor! Talk about "Frying tonight"! It's about time those two got — fired!

He throws the boots off stage and returns to Sally

Arthur (*shaking the dragon by the claw*) Thank you, Mrs Dragon! You did a good job of getting rid of those rotters! *A flaming* good job, in fact! Haw! Haw! Haw!
Merlin   And for those of you who may be concerned,
                With the nasties, demise, my wand has returned!

Merlin holds up his wand

All Hurray!

The Chorus and Dancers, as Knights, Ladies of the Court, etc., enter and fill the back. The little Page saunters on from DR, carrying Excalibur. He gives a loud sniff

Page (*to Arthur*) Fought you might be needin' this!

With a sniff, he holds out the sword

Arthur Ah! Good old Excalibur! Better late than never, what!

He goes to take the sword, but hesitates, remembering what happened the last time. He steels himself and takes the sword. To his amazement and delight, it doesn't crash to the ground. Proudly, he holds Excalibur aloft for all to see

All Hurray!
Guinevere (*delighted*) Oh, Arthur! You've managed to keep it up!
Merlin (*to all , including the audience*)
           With Morgana well and truly sorted,
           The threat to King Arthur has now been thwarted.
           Let us celebrate this joyous day —
           With a song and dance! (*To the conductor or pianist*)
           Take it away!

The music starts and they all go into a joyful song and dance

Song 15

After the song, a front cloth is lowered or the tabs close

Scene 6

A Little Knight Music

Front cloth or tabs

Squirt enters and waves to the audience

Squirt Hallo folks! Hi, kids! Well, that's it! It's nearly all over! Sad, isn't it? But as we say in Camelot — once a knight, always a knight! But once a night is enough! You've been a smashin' audience! The best we've had all evening!
Sally (*off, calling*) Yoo Hoo! Squirty!
Squirt Look out! 'Ere comes (*current personality*)!

   Sally runs on, greatly excited

Sally Squirty! 'Ave you 'eard the news?
Squirt What is it? 'Ave (*topical / local reference*)?

Sally No! It's Sir Lancelot and Lady Olivia! They're in love, and they're goin' to get married! (*Sidling up to him*) Oh, isn't that romantic, Squirty. Why don't we make it a *double*!

Squirt Good idea! I'll see you in the pub!

He moves to exit

Sally (*pulling him back*) No! I mean a double *wedding*! Lancelot and Olivia. An' — you an' me!

Squirt But I'm too young to die!

Sally (*stamping her foot, angrily*) You promised you'd marry me! You promised!

Squirt (*reluctantly*) Oh, all right then!

Sally Well, do it properly!

Sally points to the floor, Squirt gives the audience a look, then goes down on one knee

Squirt Sally! Will you marry me, and become my awful wedded wife?

Sally (*acting coy*) Oh, this is so sudden! You'll 'ave to ask my dad first.

Squirt I don't want to marry '*im*!

Sally Oh, Squirtykins! Of course I'll marry you!

She grabs his head and hugs it tightly

Guinevere and Smoulder enter. The queen wears a comical outfit that can be easily changed for the finale

Guinevere Oy! Oy! Oy! What's goin' on 'ere? (*She covers Smoulder's eyes*) Not in front of the children, *please*! What do you think this is (*current risqué film or TV programme*)?

Sally releases Squirt. He falls over and lies gasping

Sally Squirt's just asked me to marry 'im, and I've accepted!

Guinevere (*looking over at the prone Squirt*) Are you sure 'e's up to it?

Squirt staggers to his feet

Well, congratulations to you both! (*To the audience*) Now, before you go 'ome, Smoulder wants you all to sing 'er favourite song! Don't you Smoulder?

Smoulder nods

(*To someone in the front row*) You'll enjoy that, won't you? Well 'ard luck!
You're goin' to, if you want to get to the (*local pub*) before last orders! (*To all*) The song is about another little dragon, and I'm sure you all know it.
Squirt (*top audience*) And if you don't — I've got the gubbins!
Sally (*looking at him*) I thought you were walkin' a bit funny!
Squirt I mean I've got the words of the song!

The song sheet is lowered or can be brought in by the little Page or a member of the Chorus. Guinevere, Squirt, Sally and Smoulder have fun getting the audience to sing. They may even like to get some children up on to the stage

Song 16

After, the song sheet is removed and the children return to their seats. Guinevere and the others wave and shout "Bye! Ta, ta! etc." to the audience and exit. Smoulder gives a final wave, and scampers out after them

The Lights fade to Black-out

SCENE 7

The Finale

A special setting or the Courtyard scene can be used

Bright lighting

Bouncy music

All enter for the Finale Walkdown. The last to enter is King Arthur carrying Excalibur

Lancelot	The time has come to say farewell,
	And leave King Arthur's Court.
Olivia	We have enjoyed your company,
	You've all been such a sport.
Arthur	What ho, old things! It's time to go,
	So ta-ta and toodle-oo!
Guinevere	I think I'll start that lottery,
	And I sincerely 'ope — "it's you"

Squirt	One day I'll be a knight so grand,
	And sit at the big Round Table!
Sally	I 'ope you're not just a *one* night stand,
	I need you fit an' able!
Morgana	I hate you all! Compared to me,
	You're very cheap and crummy!
Mordred	Please don't call her nasty names.
	Remember — she's still my mummy!
Merlin	A "magic" audience you have all been!
	Our thanks to you now incur
	Good-night, God bless from all of us —
All	At the Court of King Arthur!

Finale Song 17

CURTAIN

FURNITURE AND PROPERTY LIST

ACT I

PROLOGUE

Personal: **Merlin**: magic wand (carried throughout)

SCENE 1

Off stage: Excalibur (**Page**)
Large shopping bag. *In it*: large oilcan, pair of knitting needles with length of chain, can of spray polish, large tin opener (**Olivia**)
Gift wrapped boxes (**Olivia**)

Personal: **Arthur**: crown, monacle (worn throughout)

SCENE 2

Off stage: Small tray. *On it:* bottles, jars and small glass phial (**Morgana**)

Personal: **Guinevere**: coin

SCENE 3

On stage: Royal Box with bell attached to right side
Two tents
Two stools
Banners, flags, etc.

Off stage: Standards (**Dancers**)
Two horses (**Lancelot** and **Mordred**)
Two lances and shields (**Lancelot** and **Mordred**)
Two battleaxes (**Squirt** and **Morgana**)
Two swords (**Squirt** and **Morgana**)
Excalibur (**Page**)
Goblet (**Olivia**)
Vending trays, etc. (**Chorus**)

Personal: **Olivia**: red scarf
Morgana: black scarf
Squirt, Sally and **Smoulder**: red pom-poms

SCENE 4

On stage: Nil

SCENE 5

On stage: Tree stump. *Behind it*: basket with real cakes
Large picnic hamper
Table-cloth. *On it*: remains of picnic

Off stage: Large Hairy Spider (**Stage Management**)
Excalibur (**Page**)
Plates and goblets (**Chorus**)
Large chicken drumstick, piece of charcoal (**Guinevere**)

ACT II

SCENE 1

On stage: Weapons, shields, flags, banners, etc.
Dais with two thrones

Off stage: Various props for chosen routine p. 45 (**Squirt, Sally** and **Smoulder**)
Excalibur (**Page**)
Apple (**Page**)
Large goblet (**Arthur**)

Personal: **Lancelot**: dagger and scabbard

SCENE 2

On stage: Nil

SCENE 3

On stage: Dented suit of armour
Cupboard. *In it*: clothes spilling out
Double bed with bedding

Off stage: Large hand mirror (**Guinevere**)
Excalibur (**Page**)

SCENE 4

On stage: Nil

SCENE 5

Off stage: Toilet brush (**Stage Management**)
Two pairs of 'smoking' boots (**Squirt**)
Excalibur (**Page**)

SCENE 6

Off stage: Song sheet (**Page, Chorus** and **Stage Management**)

SCENE 7

Off stage: Excalibur (**Arthur**)

LIGHTING PLOT

PROLOGUE

To open: *Black-out*

Cue 1   Flash. **Merlin** enters   (Page 1)
            Follow spot on **Merlin**

Cue 2   **Merlin** waves his wand at the curtains. Flash   (Page 2)
            Cut spot

ACT I, SCENE 1

To open: General exterior lighting

Cue 3   **Lancelot**: "A lady-in-waiting, perhaps."   (Page 18)
            Romantic lighting

Cue 4   Song 4 ends   (Page 18)
            Fade to black-out

ACT 1, SCENE 2

To open: Eerie lighting

Cue 5   **Morgana** and **Mordred** exit   (Page 19)
            Cross-fade to general exterior lighting

Cue 6   **Guinevere** skips out   (Page 24)
            Cross-fade to eerie spotlight on **Morgana**

Cue 7   **Morgana** exits   (Page 24)
            Fade to black-out

ACT I, SCENE 3

To open: General exterior lighting

Cue 8   At end of Song 7   (Page 34)
            Fade to black-out

ACT I, SCENE 4

To open: Eerie lighting

Cue 9   **Morgana** and **Mordred** exit   (Page 35)
             Cross-fade to general exterior lighting

Cue 10   **Squirt** and **Sally** exit   (Page 37)
             Fade to black-out

ACT I, SCENE 5

To open: General exterior lighting

Cue 11   **Lancelot** sits on the tree stump   (Page 42)
             Gradual fade

Cue 12   **Lancelot**: "… to get dark."   (Page 42)
             Bring up eerie, strange lighting

Cue 13   **Morgana** enters   (Page 43)
             Bring up green follow spot on **Morgana**

Cue 14   **Morgana**, **Mordred** and **Dancers** exit   (Page 43)
             Return to general exterior lighting

Cue 15   **Lancelot** exits   (Page 44)
             Flash of lightning. Lighting grows dark and creepy.
             Bring up green follow spot on **Morgana**

Cue 16   **Morgana** stands on the stump and raises her arms   (Page 44)
             Flash of lightning

ACT II, SCENE 1

To open: General interior lighting

Cue 17   **Lancelot**: "Very well, sire."   (Page 48)
             Lighting grows dark and sinister

Cue 18   **Lancelot** raises his head   (Page 48)
             Eerie follow spot on **Lancelot**

Cue 19   **Merlin**: (*calling, off*) "Sire! Sire!"   (Page 49)
             Instantly change to general interior lighting

Cue 20   **Lancelot**: "Certainly, sire."   (Page 49)
             Lighting grows dark and sinister

Cue 21	**Lancelot** falls into a trance *Eerie follow spot on* **Lancelot**	(Page 50)
Cue 22	**Olivia**: (*calling, off*) "Sire! Sire!" *Instantly change to general interior lighting*	(Page 50)
Cue 23	**Lancelot**: "I'm drunk on love!" *Romantic lighting*	(Page 51)
Cue 24	End of Song 11 *Fade to black-out*	(Page 51)

ACT II, SCENE 2

To open: Eerie lighting

| Cue 25 | **Morgana** and **Mordred** exit
Frosty, moonlit effect | (Page 52) |
| Cue 26 | **Smoulder** waves and exits
Fade to black-out | (Page 55) |

ACT II, SCENE 3

To open: General interior lighting

Cue 27	**Guinevere**: "*Hit it!*" *Lights dim. Follow spot on* **Guinevere**	(Page 57)
Cue 28	**Guinevere** strikes a pose as music stops *Take out spot and return to general interior lighting*	(Page 58)
Cue 29	**Arthur** and **Guinevere** snore *Lighting grows dark and eerie*	(Page 58)
Cue 30	**Lancelot** appears in archway *Eerie follow spot on* **Lancelot**	(Page 59)
Cue 31	**Arthur**: "Lancelot!" *Instantly change to general interior lighting*	(Page 59)
Cue 32	**Merlin**: "The evil Morgana!" *Flash of lightning. Lighting grows dark and sinister*	(Page 61)
Cue 33	**Morgana**: "Ha! Ha! Ha!" *Flash of lightning, followed by black-out. Allow time for* **Guinevere** *and* **Olivia** *to exit, then return to dark, sinister lighting*	(Page 61)

Cue 34   **Morgana**: … if you dare! Ha! Ha! Ha!"   (Page 62)
            Change to general interior lighting

Cue 35   **Merlin** exits   (Page 62)
            Fade to black-out

ACT II, SCENE 4

To open: Moonlit exterior lighting

Cue 36   **Morgana**: "… Ha! Ha! Ha!"   (Page 66)
            Flash of lightning

Cue 37   **Morgana** exits   (Page 66)
            Fade to black-out

ACT II, SCENE 5

To open: Spooky exterior lighting. Flash of lightning

Cue 38   After Song 14   (Page 67)
            Flash of lightning. Green follow spot on **Morgana**

Cue 39   **Morgana** exits   (Page 68)
            Flash of lightning. Cut green follow spot

Cue 40   **Arthur**: "…Tally-ho!"   (Page 68)
            Flash of lightning

Cue 41   **Morgana** enters   (Page 68)
            Green follow spot on **Morgana**

Cue 42   **Morgana**: "Now!"   (Page 70)
            Flash of lightning

Cue 43   **Merlin**: "Begone!"   (Page 70)
            Weird lights flash across stage. (Optional strobe)

Cue 44   **Ghouls** run out   (Page 71)
            Return to spooky exterior lighting

Cue 45   **Morgana** exits   (Page 71)
            Cut green follow spot

Cue 46   **Morgana** makes magic passes at **Merlin**   (Page 71)
            *Weird lights flash acrosss stage, then return to
            spooky exterior lighting*

Cue 47   Flash, explosion and smoke off   (Page 74)
              Bright general lighting

ACT II, SCENE 6

To open: General lighting

Cue 48   **Smoulder** waves and exits   (Page 77)
              Fade to black-out

ACT II, SCENE 7

To open: Full general lighting
              No cues

EFFECTS PLOT

PROLOGUE

Cue 1	After overture and house lights down *Flash and puff of smoke*	(Page 1)
Cue 2	**Merlin** waves a wand at the curtains *Flash and puff of smoke. Fanfare*	(Page 2)

ACT I

Cue 3	**Merlin**: "… strike up the band!" *Fanfare*	(Page 4)
Cue 4	**Merlin**: "… your sovereign lord!" *Louder fanfare*	(Page 4)
Cue 5	**Merlin**: "… *your sovereign lord!*" *Even louder fanfare*	(Page 5)
Cue 6	To open SCENE 3 *Fanfare*	(Page 25)
Cue 7	The crowd sing *Fanfare*	(Page 25)
Cue 8	**Merlin**: "… Queen Guinevere!" *Fanfare*	(Page 25)
Cue 9	**Merlin** bangs his wand three times *Fanfare*	(Page 28)
Cue 10	**Lancelot**: "… to get dark." *Ground mist. Unearthly sounds*	(Page 42)
Cue 11	**Morgana, Mordred** and **Dancers** exit *Fade out unearthly sounds*	(Page 43)
Cue 12	**Lancelot** exits *Roll of thunder. Ground mist*	(Page 44)

Cue 13   **Morgana** stands on the stump and raises her arms   (Page 44)
          Roll of thunder. Ground mist

ACT II

Cue 14   **Lancelot**: "Very well, sire."   (Page 48)
          Weird sounds, faintly at first, then increasing in volume

Cue 15   **Merlin**: (*calling, off*) "Sire! Sire!"   (Page 49)
          Instantly cut weird sounds

Cue 16   **Lancelot**: "Certainly, sire."   (Page 49)
          Weird sounds as before

Cue 17   **Olivia**: (*calling, off*) "Sire! Sire!   (Page 50)
          Instantly cut weird sounds

Cue 18   **Merlin**: "*Take flight!*"   (Page 60)
          Flash and puff of smoke

Cue 19   **Merlin**: "The evil Morgana!"   (Page 61)
          Roll of thunder

Cue 20   **Morgana**: "Ha! Ha! Ha!"   (Page 61)
          Roll of thunder. Weird sounds during black-out.
          Fade out sounds when Lights come up

Cue 21   **Morgana**: "… Ha! Ha! Ha!"   (Page 66)
          Roll of thunder. Howling wind and weird sounds that
          continue into the next scene with ground mist

Cue 22   After Song 14   (Page 67)
          Roll of thunder

Cue 23   **Morgana** exits   (Page 68)
          Fade out wind and weird sounds

Cue 24   **Arthur**: "… Tally-ho!"   (Page 68)
          Crash of thunder

Cue 25   **Morgana**: "Now!"   (Page 70)
          Roll of thunder. Ground mist

Cue 26   The **Ghouls** advance on **Arthur** and **Lancelot**   (Page 70)
          Flash and puff of smoke

Cue 27	**Merlin**: "Begone!" *Flash*	(Page 70)
Cue 28	**Morgana** makes magic passes at **Merlin** *Flash*	(Page 71)
Cue 29	**Morgana**: "Your killing powers I know *invoke!*" *Dragon's roar, gradually increasing in volume. Blinding* *flash and jet of smoke from off* L. *Ground mist*	(Page 72)
Cue 30	**Morgana**: "Destroy them all!" *Dragon's roar*	(Page 72)
Cue 31	During **Lancelot**'s fight with dragon *Dragon's roar*	(Page 73)
Cue 32	**Merlin**: "… has a score to settle!" *Dragon's roar*	(Page 73)
Cue 33	**Dragon** exits after **Morgana** and **Mordred** *Blinding flash, loud explosion and cloud of smoke* *from off*	(Page 74)